THE MULTIPLICATION FACTOR

16 Truths about Partnering with God in Business and Life

MARK WALKER

FOREWORD AND CONCLUSION BY JOHNNY ENLOW

Copyright © 2023 by Mark Walker

All rights reserved. No part of this publication may be reproduced, distributed, or transmitted in any form or by any means, including photocopying, recording, or other electronic or mechanical methods, without the prior written permission of the publisher, except in the case of brief quotations embodied in critical reviews and certain other noncommercial uses permitted by copyright law. For permission requests, write to the publisher at the address below.

All Scripture quotations are from the New King James Version®. Copyright © 1982 by Thomas Nelson. Used by permission. All rights reserved.

Cover design by Mackenna Cotten
Photo by Unsplash

Fedd Books
P.O. Box 341973
Austin, TX 78734

www.thefeddagency.com

Published in association with The Fedd Agency, Inc., a literary agency.

ISBN: 978-1-957616-45-2
eISBN: 978-1-957616-46-9

LCCN: 2023909389

Printed in the United States of America

DEDICATION

This book is dedicated to my family and wife. My wife, the love of my life for over forty years, has always encouraged and strengthened me in my walk with God. She has a heart of generosity to freely give her time and energy to our family, friends, and various ministries. Pam was the first person with whom I shared my vision of opening a business to support the gospel, and she thought it was a great idea. Later we were married, and we partnered with God to advance His Kingdom. She has always been there supporting me, even on my worst days. This book never would have been finished without her involvement and encouragement. Together we've had an amazing life walking with God.

One of the reasons I wanted to write this book was to leave a legacy for my children and grandchildren, so I also dedicate this book to my daughters, Larisa and Crystal, and their families, especially my five grandsons. I know you all have a special place in God's heart, and He desires to partner with you in this life to become a blessing to others. Adam, last but not least, you are anointed to steward what God has done with Walker's Furniture, and I've already started seeing that my ceiling is truly becoming your floor.

Johnny, thank you for writing a foreword and conclusion for this book and for being such a great example of someone always ready to advance the Kingdom of God. Without your encouragement, likely this book would not exist.

Elizabeth, thank you for all your ideas. Your added suggestions made this book more user-friendly. You have always encouraged me in everything I do.

Restore7 team, thanks for all your hard work to take this book to a level of excellence. Travis, Jason, and Mariah, thanks for all you did to help my writing flow and expertise.

Walker's Employees, thank you for so many years of hard work and dedication to make Walker's Furniture successful—especially the Walker's administration and management teams. Your faithfulness to our company vision has helped position us for success in every way.

TABLE OF CONTENTS

FOREWORD

As a pastor I often ran into people with a great love for Jesus but a wrong understanding about serving Him. People almost always think that if they are going to make a difference in God's Kingdom, they need to "go into ministry." They rarely recognize the vital connection between their work or business and the advancement of the Kingdom.

There are some understandable reasons for this. Christians have often noticed how money and business can be corrupting, but instead of bringing God's presence and character into the business world, they have either compartmentalized their lives to keep their work and spiritual selves separate or left that sector of society completely. After all, Jesus did teach about the dangers of loving money. So many in the church have decided that the best way to avoid that danger is to avoid business and wealth altogether. Instead of becoming influencers in the marketplace—or anywhere in society—they have retreated into a Christian subculture and then tried to reach "secular society" from the outside.

Unfortunately, this perspective has a way of paralyzing people who long to be fruitful in God's Kingdom. I've heard many believers apologize for working to pay the bills until they can one day serve God by going into full-time ministry. Somehow the church has lost the understanding that when God's people carry His presence and ways, true full-time ministry invades every area of society. Christians have focused on working for God within or from the church without any understanding of how to do business with God everywhere.

As I've noted in my books, the framework for understanding how God is working in this world calls for His people to bring their Kingdom influence into every major area of society—what I refer to as the "Seven Mountains": government, education, media, economy, arts and entertainment, religion, and family. You are likely reading this book because you are called to the "Mountain of Economy."

Because Christians have historically focused most of their attention on the "Mountain of Religion"—working within the church to focus on influencing people spiritually—we have watched society become ever more secular and instead turned our attention to being taken out of this corrupt world when Jesus returns. This is a paradigm that needs to be corrected. God's purpose is not to take His people out of the world; it's to send us into every aspect of it until His glory covers the earth (Habakkuk 2:14).

My wife and I have adopted this as the mission of our ministry, Restore7, because the church is in such great need of seeing God's Kingdom differently from how it has long been defined. We believe there is much more need today for anointing in business and society's other mountains than there is for anointing behind the pulpit. (There is a need for anointing in the pulpit too, but we already give plenty of attention to that.)

Many who finally become "full-time ministers" are surprised that their ministry seems to go nowhere without funds. Then they turn around and appeal to people in the business world they just left, asking them to fund their holy work, not realizing that funding ministry and demonstrating God's heart in businesses is just as holy. Many "full-time ministers" were positioned to be a means of God's Kingdom provision but thought it was more spiritual to be in need of it. Our Kingdom assignment is to go into all the mountains of society. We need God's Kingdom agents and His resources everywhere—not just to help the local church grow bigger and better but also to demonstrate God's heart in every corner of the world. We have a massive reformation assignment in every sphere of society.

Society needs God's anointed people in every aspect of our world.

This is where anointed businesspeople come in. Compared to the Kingdom assignment set before us, financiers are scarce. We need huge armies of people who understand that their calling is to earn money to fund ministry. We also need those same people to be ministers where they are. Most of the world will not be drawn to the churches' glory. But people will be drawn to the glory of God at work in His people in business, as well as in government, media, education, arts and entertainment, and families.

The Lord has given me a picture of a tremendous explosion of Kingdom financiers—anointed multimillionaires who know their calling for the historic assignment before us. God is going to raise up many who are able to earn enormous amounts of money without loving it for its own sake. They will see themselves as channels of blessing for the world rather than as reservoirs of wealth for themselves. God has already begun doing this—you will read about one couple who has taken up that assignment in this book, and there are others out there—but they will only increase in the months and years to come. Those who are faithful in a little will be given more in order to promote His comprehensive Kingdom work.

Almost everything God does on earth is intended to be done with and through His children who understand their roles as ambassadors of His Kingdom. And much of it needs funding. God wants to rebuild cities and nations—to eradicate diseases, end famines, quiet wars, establish justice, heal wounds, and recreate societies to reflect His Kingdom. Of course, this requires people who reflect His Kingdom and embody His ways, not just in the church but everywhere else. That's why every calling is important, including the calling to make money in business.

This is a far cry from the prosperity gospel. Scripture strongly warns against seeking wealth for its own sake, prioritizing it above God's Kingdom, making it an idol, and distorting its legitimate uses. But Scripture also gives us numerous examples of God blessing His people financially and promising to increase what they receive so they can increase what they give. He wants good stewards in His Kingdom to use their gifts to become greater and greater channels of financial blessing. Contrary to many teachings over the centuries, poverty is not spiritual. Giving is. And God wants many of His people to grow financially so they can become more extravagant givers.

The story you are about to read illustrates this paradigm beautifully. It's the story of a man who felt ignited one night with the simple desire to be a generous giver toward Christian ministries and projects. He didn't even have a business at the time, but he knew God had planted a calling into his heart. He dreamed of bearing Kingdom fruitfulness by funding the good news of Jesus and His ways.

I have highly anticipated writing a foreword to Mark's book because he and Pam are such wonderful prototypes of what God is looking for on the Mountain of Economy. Because the Seven Mountain message of advancing and exhibiting God's Kingdom in the seven primary spheres of society is a relatively new way of looking at things (although the principles behind it are as old as Scripture), we need examples of what this looks like in actual lives. Mark and Pam Walker are great examples to follow.

I believe this story can be life-changing for many. God turned Mark and Pam's simple but genuine desire to be Kingdom financiers into reality. From the beginning they were in it together, combining their wisdom, discernment, and faith to take bold steps that required miraculous provision. As you will see, God came through every single time.

This story needs to be out there. Mark drops golden keys of wisdom throughout. I believe absorbing them and putting them into practice can transform the way you think about God and His Kingdom.

Though this story is told from Mark's perspective, you will easily see what Pam has brought to the table too. Their victories are the result of unity that, as in any marriage, did not always come easily but was always richly rewarded. My prayer is that you will allow yourself to read slowly, asking the Holy Spirit to speak and catch all the hidden treasures in Mark and Pam's journey—a journey of becoming trusted ministers of wealth in God's Kingdom.

Mark is not a pastor or even a speaker (yet), but he has a gift for breaking every lesson he learned into precise, bite-size nuggets of truth.

His wisdom comes from five decades of doing business with God. This business relationship faced many crises, but Mark and Pam recognized these junctures as important moments. These were when those golden nuggets were revealed and developed. Mark brilliantly calls them truths about partnering with God; I call them rewards of obedience. Whatever you call them, they are available to everyone.

Mark is a humble man who is understated in just about every way. He admits to many mistakes and failures throughout his career, but as he demonstrates, the point is not to be perfect—it's to be faithful, to notice when you've left God out of the picture or missed what He was saying, and to learn what you can from those experiences and keep returning to that faithful partnership. God always keeps His promises and invites us to grow in our understanding of how He works. Mark and Pam are a great picture of what that partnership with God looks like.

As we partner with God, we really do have an "unfair" advantage. This God sustains a business when the giants of competition are all around, when the market crashes, when a pandemic changes the rules of success, and in any other scenario of adversity. God is not limited by anything, and He walks His people through all the challenges of life from the perspective of His measureless resources, not our limited abilities. The story that follows illustrates how Mark and Pam relied on Him, received His blessings, and have become a blessing to their family, their company, their community, and God's Kingdom. By learning from their experiences, you may find God writing a story just as remarkable through you.

—Johnny Enlow

INTRODUCTION

Multiplication

God's plan from the beginning has always been to bless people so they can become blessings. You can easily see that God entered the covenant with Abraham and His descendants to be a blessing to nations. Isaac experienced a hundredfold increase during a drought. Joseph and Daniel started basically as slaves and were promoted to key positions alongside their kings. Esther was hated and despised in her community, yet she became a queen with great influence. Throughout Scripture, you see God's heart to multiply His people's influence in order to help others.

Jesus came to manifest God's heart, to multiply His goodness and glory here on earth. He came not to judge the world but to save the world. Jesus saw that five thousand were hungry, so He instructed his disciples to distribute what they had, five loaves and two fish. It multiplied so that everyone was fed. There were even twelve baskets left over—that's more than a hundredfold increase!

When the disciples fished all night and caught nothing, Jesus directed them to launch the boats and to let their nets down. As soon as they did so, they caught so many fish that their nets nearly broke. They filled two boats so full that they began sinking. Again we read about more than a hundredfold increase as God reveals His heart to multiply His goodness and provision to a needy world.

After the resurrection of Jesus, some of the disciples were fishing again, and Jesus asked them if they had any food. When they answered no, Jesus told them to cast the net on the right side of the boat and they would find some. Simon Peter and the others dragged the net to land and found it overflowing with large fish. The net didn't break even though there were so many large fish. Jesus revealed His Kingdom strategies for multiplication even after the disciples' confusion and discouragement because of the cross.

I believe all these miracles reveal God's heart to multiply His Kingdom. The disciples who followed Jesus continuously saw how generous He was and how He multiplied grace and favor in the lives of those who freely stepped out in faith to release His generosity.

This book captures some of my story; it's filled with examples of God's multiplication in one man's life.

Someone recently asked me why I started a business at a young age and what motivated me to keep growing it. The simple answer is—*God.* He promised to partner with me in business to help release the gospel, the good news, around the world. This book is about God's faithfulness in partnering with my wife and me to build a business to fulfill our destiny.

From the beginning I had faith that with God, anything is possible. If I partnered with God, He would not only provide the seed for me to start my business, but He would also multiply the seed I sowed as our business grew. I believed our business would be successful, yet what God did was miraculous beyond anything I could have ever done in my ability and strength. As I look back, it is easy to see how faithful God was to empower me in business to establish His Kingdom. As I stepped out in faith, God supplied great employees, amazing locations, and new business strategies so our business would grow and we could be very generous.

God is always looking for people with loyal hearts to show Himself strong, those who will lean on Him in partnership, walking with Him to influence the world. I learned early on to stop trying to fit God into my plans and to just fit my life into His plans. As I sought to do His will through my business, God continually blessed what I put my hands to and revealed His heart to multiply His Kingdom. I've discovered it is so important to always remember that God is more concerned with your relationship with Him than your ability to prosper, because fullness of life is experienced as God's love flows through your life.

Over the years, I developed a deep desire to walk with Him every day of my life. We all need to continuously strengthen our relationship and walk with the Lord to build His Kingdom. We should never get discouraged, even if everything gets shaken around us. God is always with us.

Remember David and Ziklag from 1 Samuel. After David and his men lost everything, including their families, David's men talked about stoning him. But David strengthened himself in the Lord and remembered all the Lord had done for him. He sought the Lord and inquired whether he should pursue this troop. When God told him to go after them, and David obeyed, they recovered everything they had lost and more. When it looked as if they had lost everything, God turned their circumstances around and multiplied their flocks.

Before David became king, he had to learn how to strengthen himself in the Lord and believe God's narrative, not the one he was currently experiencing. No matter the circumstances, I encourage you to lean into God and follow His direction. Build up your faith, knowing that God is with you and that He will fight for you.

This book is the testimony of how God supernaturally blessed the business He directed my wife, Pam, and me to open as we set our affections on building and advancing His Kingdom. We hope our testimony will encourage you to realize that anything is possible with God. His promise through His Word—to give me the power to get wealth—inspired and motivated me to open a business in my 20s with almost no money or business ideas. Within twenty years we went from nothing to a multi-million-dollar company that exceeded our abilities and skills. Now, after more than forty years, we own several of our retail locations with no debt, and we are co-owners of a successful chain of furniture stores with annual sales of $70 million. Through four-and-a-half decades in life and business, God revealed how faithful He is to fulfill His promises.

Pam and I can now look back and see how God did all the heavy lifting. We were just tools in His hands as He taught us foundational truths from His Word. He provided us with resources and told us what kind of business to open. When we started, He continually gave us new strategies, great locations, and amazing people to come alongside us. These sixteen truths were the building blocks of our success as we experienced miracle after miracle.

This is the story of those miracles.

TRUTH ONE

Jesus gave His life so we can walk together in this life.

"I have come that they may have life, and that they may have it more abundantly."

—JOHN 10:10

In my senior year of high school, months before I graduated and as I planned to go to college to pursue my dreams, I found the greatest treasure in the world. This changed everything in my life, including those dreams. I suddenly had a purpose and a plan.

In so many ways, that purpose and plan hasn't changed.

Before I found this treasure and purpose, however, I was living an ordinary life. In many ways, my childhood was normal. I went to school and enjoyed playing sports, as many kids do. But as with many homes, mine became somewhat dysfunctional. My mom spent many childbearing years in bed from pregnancies and a bad back, so I was raised by a nanny who came in the morning, made meals, and got me ready to walk to my Catholic grade school. My dad was a successful architect, but he spent a lot of time with friends on weekends. I don't remember being close to either of my parents.

In my junior year of high school my parents divorced, and my life went completely off track. I became self-centered and lived as though everything were about me—what I needed and wanted to do. My sole desire was to enjoy and experience life, so I cared only for my needs. Every weekend was a party, yet deep down I was miserable.

In the spring of my senior year everything changed. A friend talked to me about how Jesus had totally changed his life. I learned that Jesus came to give His life so we could have His life, about how God gave us His Son, Jesus, so that He could live in us and through us. That is the great mystery—Jesus living in us with the expectation of His goodness flowing through us!

I surrendered my life to Jesus that day. I repented and asked God for forgiveness. I was born again—radically converted—as I encountered God in a new way. Suddenly the weight of my past mistakes fell from my shoulders. I could tell that everything had changed.

I had a new start at life.

My chief goal became wanting to spend all my extra time reading the Bible and praying. Even on spring break, which was the following week, I spent most of the time reading Scripture, praying, and going to charismatic meetings that were very different from what I had experienced at my Catholic church.

God was transforming me on the inside. It felt that I had a new beginning; I was no longer thinking all about my needs and wants. I was excited about living for Jesus, serving Him, doing His will, and discovering what that looked like. I knew God had called me into His Kingdom, and I wanted to understand His plans and purposes for my life. Just as Jesus laid down His life for me, I had a desire to lay down my life for others. Some way, somehow, I wanted to make a difference and help people.

Truth One

PARTNERING WITH GOD

When I went to college, one of my first new Christian thoughts was to be wary of money. I had seen how money in many ways had corrupted my dad, so I didn't think I wanted to have a lot of it. With my Catholic upbringing and mentality, I assumed I could get closer to God only when I was poor.

My goal, as I began my first semester at the University of Washington, was to decide what to do with my life. I would eventually need to make decisions regarding my major, but immediately I would need to decide what kind of life I wanted to lead at school. I could follow the crowd or live for Christ. Fortunately, I found a Christian group of college kids and young married couples who were meeting off campus a couple of times a week—and they were all excited about living for God.

During those searching days when I sought to know how to serve God, I went on a four-week missionary trip to southwest Alaska and helped kids with summer Bible camps. It was a great experience, but I did not feel called to missionary work.

In my sophomore year I had to choose and apply for my major. I wanted to make a good decision because many students who changed majors as juniors went to school for an extra year, a total of five years. My goal was to be finished in four. I thought about a business degree—both of my grandfathers and my dad were successful businessmen, and I was very good at math—but I wanted to make a difference for Christ. I wanted to help people—to lay my life down for others just as Jesus laid His life down for me and the world. He did not come to earth to be served but to serve, so that was my goal. And according to my Catholic background, where I had learned about priests and sisters who took vows of poverty, I thought money would hinder my walk with Him.

A friend told me about physical and occupational therapy and how you could help people overcome physical and mental handicaps. Feeling the pressure to decide quickly and without much research, I applied for occupational therapy as my major and was accepted.

The winter of my junior year, the direction and purpose of my life changed forever. I will never forget our church meeting in the basement of a home with about fifty people and a visiting pastor from a small church in Canada. The pastor was also a businessman, who left an impression. He said the greatest need in the church was finances. He noted that lack of funding hindered the spread of the gospel around the world.

"There are many anointed ministers doing a great work for God," the pastor said, "but they don't have enough financial support to accomplish what God has called them to do."

Then he began speaking a prophetic word to us. He looked at us with an intense expression.

"God is going to raise up and anoint people like you in all kinds of occupations and businesses to support the gospel financially."

The pastor told us that God would give people great business ideas and witty inventions and promote them to key positions in influential companies. As owners and CEOs, many would build great companies to finance the spread of the gospel. He said God would partner with these people, and then he quoted Deuteronomy 8:18: "And you shall remember the Lord your God, for it is He who gives you power to get wealth, that He may establish His covenant."

I had never heard that before.

God, the creator of this universe, is looking for people to partner with in business to advance His Kingdom.

As he talked, it felt as if a blanket had been draped over me. Suddenly I knew this was my purpose and destiny. I wanted to support the gospel in a big way. I felt like jumping up and saying, "Yes! That's what I want to do!" I had no money, experience, or business ideas—but I knew this word was for me.

From that moment on I was committed to starting a business to help finance the gospel, and I believed God would partner with me and show me what to do.

With that prophetic word that night, I started on a new path.

> *I wanted to surrender my life to gain His life.*

A DESTINY REVEALED

God has given us His instruction booklet in the Bible. He speaks to us through His holy Word. Knowing this, I looked for every passage in the Bible about how people entered into covenant with God to do His will and advance His Kingdom through business. I discovered more examples than I imagined I would.

I read about Abraham, who was told by God that he and his family would be blessed so they could be a blessing to nations.

I read about how Isaac obeyed God and had a hundredfold increase during a drought, then how Jacob greatly prospered after receiving a dream from God about putting spotted rods in the watering troughs.

Joseph went from a slave to overseeing Potiphar's house, then from prison to the palace, becoming Pharaoh's right-hand man.

Solomon went from building the temple to being asked by God what he wanted. Solomon did not ask for riches but for wisdom to guide the people. God gave him both—great wealth and wisdom.

Story after story in Scripture reveals God's heart to prosper His people in all things so that they could be a blessing to others and advance His Kingdom. I didn't have to start a business to become rich; I could start a business to finance the spread of the gospel around the world.

God began revealing to me that night how much He loved me. He chose me and had a plan for my life, even when I felt I had nothing to offer. He was opening my eyes to see that we would partner together in this business, that He would direct my steps and give me success. I learned that Jesus is our inheritance, that we all have a calling and purpose to advance the Kingdom, that we can partner with His power's exceeding greatness to do the impossible through faith. I started dreaming about giving at least 30 percent of my income to God and Kingdom ministries.

I will never forget that night when God revealed my destiny to me—when in the middle of that meeting in the basement, the visiting pastor looked at our young congregation and said God would pour out His anointing on His people in their occupations to help finance the gospel. He prophesied that God would give people the power to get wealth to advance His Kingdom. We would get new ideas for business and inventions that would totally change how business was done. God had a plan and was looking for people to partner with Him to finance His purposes. I immediately knew that word was for me and instantly committed to it in my heart.

Little did I know that my future wife was in that meeting. I later heard that one of my friends in that meeting was among the first twenty employees to work for Microsoft and had a very successful career. God was looking for people to say yes, and many of us who were there answered. I believe God is still looking for people to partner with Him in their occupations to help finance His plans of releasing more of His Kingdom into the earth.

MAKING A DIFFERENCE

Even though I had found a purpose in my life, I didn't have a plan. But that didn't matter to God. I've learned that if you set your heart and affection on advancing His Kingdom, you will be amazed at what He will do as He anoints your ability and talents. Paul said that the only thing restricting us is our affections (2 Corinthians 6:12).

God saw my heart and came alongside me to labor with me in business. I am convinced that His eyes are still running to and fro throughout the whole earth to show Himself strong on behalf of those whose hearts are loyal to Him (2 Chronicles 16:9). He is looking for anyone with a willing heart to serve people and advance His Kingdom in one of the Seven Mountains of influence: media, family, arts and entertainment, economy, religion, education, and government.[1] Whatever occupation you have in one of these mountains, you can carry God's anointing to pour out His love and presence into your sphere of influence and release His light.

God looks at everyone's heart. Whatever your education or social status, whether at your highest or lowest point in life, He looks at your heart. He will often choose the foolish and weak things of the world to confound and shame the wise. Our lives are testimonies of how He can take people with nothing and bless them so they can make a difference.

Titus 2:14 says Jesus gave His life to redeem us from every lawless deed and to purify for Himself His own special people, zealous of good works. Yes, we all have an opportunity to carry God's glory and goodness into our occupation, business, or sphere of influence. I believe the fullness of life is when Jesus lives in us and through us to advance our Father's Kingdom by serving others. I hope this book will help you realize that you too can make a difference. With God, all things are possible!

A QUOTE ON PARTNERSHIP

By accepting God as our partner, no limit can be placed on what can be achieved. But God is no remote partner, satisfied if we go to church on Sunday and drop some religious money—the small change that goes to church—on the platter. He isn't overwhelmed if we read the Bible occasionally and obey the Golden Rule. That isn't active Christianity, but just a half-hearted way of getting along.

When we go into partnership with God, we've got a Partner closer and more active than any human partner we can ever get. He participates fully in everything we let Him do, and when we start putting on airs and thinking we're doing it with our own head of steam, He can set us down quicker and harder than a thunderbolt.

There's nothing dull about being in partnership with God. God has set me down with some terrific jolts from time to time, but when my attitude has improved, and He has seen genuine repentance, He is the only Partner Who can supply total forgiveness. (R. G. LeTourneau, *Mover of Men and Mountains.* LeTourneau was a business magnate, philanthropist, and inventor who held nearly three hundred patents.)

QUESTIONS TO CONSIDER

God has wired each of us to live in relationship and cooperation with Him. I've certainly been most fulfilled when I've lived this way.

If you have not received God's gift of salvation through His Son Jesus, are you willing to pray a sincere and simple prayer now, inviting Him into your heart and life as Savior and Lord? This will forever be the greatest and most important prayer you will ever pray.

If you have already invited Him into your heart, are you willing to surrender your life to Him in a new way today, to gain the life He has for you?

"You know the grace of our Lord Jesus Christ, that though He was rich, yet for your sakes He became poor, that you through His poverty might become rich."

—2 CORINTHIANS 8:9

TRUTH TWO

God loves to take the weak and make them strong.

". . . by which have been given to us exceedingly great and precious promises, that through these you may be partakers [partners] of the divine nature."

—2 PETER 1:4

There are three main modes or levels of existence: survival, success, and significance. My story starts with survival mode, then goes through success mode into significance. None of these levels has anything to do with how much money you have or what you've accomplished. You reach a life of significance when you step into the fullness of your calling and purpose—when God's blessings continually flow through you to those He directs you to give to or serve.

This can happen in many ways. For example, a school custodian encouraging students, a senator representing the people in his or her state with integrity, a professional athlete impacting fans, a radio announcer serving listeners, an artist creating inspiring murals, a nurse carrying God's presence and love into a hospital, a teacher shaping the lives of students—and even a young man opening a small unfinished furniture store in Spokane to finance the gospel.

God has a plan for everyone's life to make a difference, but first we must invite Him in, learn from Him, and walk with Him.

SURVIVAL MODE

In survival mode people live from day to day and month to month, making just enough money to get by and survive. Their bills are usually higher than their monthly income, and they tend to develop a poverty mindset. They want to hold onto everything. They focus on themselves and their problems and have no time to think about anyone else.

Survival mode can easily result from difficult life circumstances such as disasters, health issues, divorce, and debt. Whether in business or life, anyone can find himself or herself in survival mode regardless of income. Howard Hughes was once one of the richest men in the world, yet he lived the last part of his life in total seclusion because of his paranoia of losing it all. This fear of loss overcame him, and he spent all his energy just trying to survive.

The good news is that Jesus gave His life to give us life. He became poor so we might become rich (2 Corinthians 8:9). He came to proclaim liberty to captives, to preach the gospel to the poor, and to heal the brokenhearted. As you set your eyes on His provision and trust Him to meet your needs, He will help you break free from the fear of circumstances and the bondage of wealth's trappings.

During my college days I was in survival mode. I had very little income, yet I knew God had a plan for my future, so I trusted that He would guide me into His plans for my life and occupation. I determined that whatever I put my hand to, I would do to the best of my ability as unto Him. I endeavored always to listen, look, and expect Him to show me my next steps. Even though I was in survival mode, I wanted to start giving to help advance His Kingdom, so I was led to pay off all debt and not charge anything on credit cards if I could not pay it off at the end of the month. Most importantly, I set my heart on financially supporting what I believed God cared about.

God wanted me to break free from the survival mode, step into success, and live a life of significance. He wants that for you too. It has been His plan from the beginning to bless people so they can then choose to become a blessing.

God has a plan for everyone's life to make a difference.

SUCCESS MODE

There are many levels of success and many opinions about what success looks like. The world defines success in terms of attaining wealth and holding a position that causes people to look up to you. In the eyes of the world, successful people have good jobs and a steady income that allows them to pay their bills and have some money left over at the end of each month. But it's easy to become preoccupied with maintaining and/or increasing one's level of success.

You have choices to make about what to do with the extra— vacations, houses, cars, investments, hobbies, clothing, and so on. Because everyone wants to improve his or her life and circumstances, there are potential temptations and trials at this level, making it hard to maintain success with joy and peace for any length of time. It is easy to become convinced that you don't have enough and need more to be safe and happy. You start trusting in your accomplishments and what you've accumulated.

Success is good, but God wants it to lead to something more—for you to become a reflection of His goodness and to bring His solutions. He is more concerned about your inner self than your outer self. God wants the condition of your heart to bring you peace and joy while you fulfill what you were created to do. As Scripture says, "The blessing of the Lord makes one rich, and He adds no sorrow with it" (Proverbs 10:22).

The path to success comes with many traps and pitfalls. One of these is the deceitfulness of riches, which can easily choke your purpose and get you off course, especially in your relationship with God. It can slow you down or prevent you from fulfilling His plans for your life.

In pursuing God's purpose, I needed to know my motive for success and develop core values concerning finances. My picture of prosperity would impact every decision I made. I was not trying to obtain a level of success for others to see and be impressed by.

The mother of two of Jesus's disciples asked if her sons could sit on each side of Him in His Kingdom. Jesus's answer was amazing: not everyone would get equal shares. He saw success so differently from the world's definitions. He explained that the world's rulers lord their status over others and exercise great authority. But in the Kingdom, those who want to be great need to become servants, just as He had come to serve rather than to be served (Matthew 20:20–28). He never mentioned how successful His followers had to be or what they needed to do for Him. He was very clear: If we want to be recognized and sit at His side, we need to serve others and give our lives away. That's how fullness of life comes.

Kingdom success looks different from worldly success. Jesus clearly shows that success is not what you accumulate, nor is it a position in which others serve you. In His Kingdom success flows to us and through us to help others. As a business owner, I prioritized serving our customers, employees, and vendors with the main goal of supporting the gospel so others would experience God's goodness.

> *Success is good, but God wants it to lead to something more.*

A LIFE OF SIGNIFICANCE

A life of significance is the most rewarding mode of existence because God flows through us to fulfill our purpose in doing His will. It is fun and fulfilling. The Holy Spirit empowers us and reveals how we can bear fruit and impact our spheres of influence. He promises to bless us in life and business as we partner with Him every step of the way. We look for opportunities to influence individuals, cities, and nations—to change the world to be a better place for everyone, on earth as it is in heaven.

When you are living a life of significance, you want to advance God's Kingdom by advancing His love however you can. You want to make a difference and will lay down your life to do it. It is so rewarding because when you lose your life, you gain His life, which is the most fulfilling thing you can experience this side of heaven.

I am convinced that everyone was created to advance the Kingdom of God—to make a difference in people's lives, to make this world a better place so it better reflects His Kingdom—and there are many ways to do it. But it is a battle to advance through these levels of life.

It's very easy to make mistakes and missteps. At every level of success there are new obstacles to overcome. Once you break out of survival mode, you encounter many traps and distractions in success mode because the enemy wants to keep you in survival mode. He will deceive and distract you from your purpose in life and do everything he can to turn your attention to your problems and cause you to fear.

"Enter by the narrow gate," Jesus said, "for wide is the gate and broad is the way that leads to destruction, and there are many who go in by it. Because narrow is the gate and difficult is the way which leads to life, and there are few who find it" (Matthew 7:13–14).

This passage is not talking about how hard it is to find the path to heaven. It speaks about how hard it is to walk in fullness of life here on earth. The enemy will do everything he can to steal, kill, and destroy your love, joy, and peace. He wants to distract you from your purpose—to get your eyes on your circumstances and problems and cause distance between you and your true source of life.

Fullness of life comes from living a life of significance as God defines it. Our inheritance is partnering with Jesus, the King of kings, doing His will throughout our lives. Jesus wants to co-labor with you so you can have a life of abundance without regard for the world's standard of success, which is defined by financial results.

No matter where you are in life right now—whether you're financially broke, physically disabled, living through a tragedy, or have a limited education—God is able to give you a life of significance because He loves to take the weak and make them strong. He wants to meet you where you are and flow to and through you so that you will break out of survival mode. If you are very successful yet trapped in your circumstances and trying to maintain your success, He wants to lift you out of that futility. If you are working nonstop, worried that you could lose all you've accomplished and accumulated, remember that true, lasting success comes from living for the Lord of Hosts to advance His Kingdom here on earth.

ALL THINGS ARE POSSIBLE

God loves to turn an impossible situation around with seemingly impossible circumstances and unlikely people. Throughout the Bible are amazing stories of people overcoming overwhelming odds because they knew God was with them and they were doing His will.

I love the story about Jonathan turning to his servant and telling him that nothing can restrain the Lord from saving by many or by few (1 Samuel 14). Because they believed, they both climbed a hill and defeated an army. Because Jonathan understood that God changes everything, he did not allow his circumstances to undermine his faith. He knew God's desire to protect His people and trusted that God would totally back him up. God shook the earth as the two men stood against all odds, causing great confusion in the Philistines' camp and driving them out of the region.

Gideon believed he was the weakest member of the weakest family, but God sent an angel to tell him he was a mighty man (Judges 6:12). Gideon was a mighty man because he believed and remembered the miracles God performed to deliver Israel out of Egypt. He had faith in God.

God had to remind him that he was a mighty man and that He was with him. Gideon was hiding in fear, but once he was convinced God was with him, he stepped out in faith. He agreed to reduce his army from ten thousand to three hundred men so the world would know that the victory was God's. All it took was faith to believe God was with him as a deliverer and protector. What looked like an unfair advantage for the Midianites quickly became an easy victory for Gideon's three hundred.

Jonathan and Gideon are examples of faithful men making a difference for God. They decided to make their lives significant for the glory of Christ. The same applies to our lives.

Look at more examples in God's Word:

Moses, one obedient man, led the children of Israel out of bondage and to the promised land.

Joseph, a prisoner, became Pharaoh's right-hand man.

David, a shepherd boy, defeated Goliath and eventually became Israel's greatest king—a passionate man who built a place to worship God in His presence.

Daniel, a prisoner of war and a servant, became the right-hand man of three kings.

Many of Jesus' disciples were uneducated men with honorable professions who became apostles of the early church.

God's desire has always been to anoint the weak and foolish for lives of significance.

Early in my life I knew I had to see that all things are possible with God and establish that truth in my heart. I had to start visualizing the positive outcomes. What happened to our business can be attributed only to God. I know it was not because of my ability.

Fullness of life comes from living a life of significance as God defines it.

SETTING US FREE

Jesus demonstrated God's heart toward the weak and foolish by healing all who came to Him.

He fed thousands and ministered to those with broken hearts. Many Christians believe Jesus was crucified only to forgive our sins, and it's true that this is a wonderful, eternal benefit of His crucifixion and resurrection, but He came for so much more. He was crucified and resurrected so that whoever believes in his or her heart that God raised Him from the dead can be raised from selfish ambitions, corruption, and darkness. Whatever your situation, however bad it is, God can raise you up out of it.

Scripture says that "whoever calls on the name of the Lord shall be saved" (Romans 10:13). *Saved* means to be made whole, to be healed, to do well, and to persevere. Jesus died to break all bondage and every curse that's holding us back. God sent His Son so that many would believe and then walk in His resurrection power—continually being transformed into His image, no longer bound to the world but walking in relationship with the King in peace, health, and prosperity. Jesus came to set us free from the bonds that hold us back so that we can break out of survival mode and then, through His resurrection power, walk in significance.

After one of the weakest moments of his life, when his feet were beaten with rods, Paul received a beating of thirty-nine stripes and was thrown into prison. His response? He was heard worshiping and singing praise to God at midnight. He set his affections on God and not on his circumstances, and of course, God showed up! An angel came, the prison doors opened, and Paul walked out healed and unhindered. I am convinced he was worshiping because he knew his success was not dependent on his circumstances. It came through his faith in his covenant relationship with God.

I will never forget the testimony I heard at least twenty-five years ago from Peter Daniels, who at age twenty-seven was an illiterate bricklayer with a rough background of drinking and bar fights. Then he met the Lord at a Billy Graham crusade. The way he tells it, two dreams were birthed in his heart that day. He wanted to give away a lot of money, and he wanted to influence the world dramatically. He tapped into God's power and became a multimillionaire through real estate investments. He began traveling around America, encouraging Christians to dream big with God.

The enemy is not particularly bothered about how many people get saved at a crusade. He comes to destroy people's faith to walk in Jesus's resurrection power and live a life of significance. His goal is to keep you in survival mode or striving to be a "success." He does not want Christians living a life of significance because that's what makes a difference in this world. He wants to prevent as many as he can from walking in God's power and authority and impacting their sphere of influence as Peter Daniels did.

When we understand that God's desire is to strengthen the weak in the world and put to shame the mighty, it is easier to step out in faith to do something great. When we opened our business, we were so small that our competition didn't even notice us. But we chose to keep believing

God and continued pursuing a life of significance. We did not stop and try to figure out how we would buy another house, buy a new car, or pay off our existing bills. We just trusted God, His promise, and His ability to lead us.

When you set your affection on a big vision of advancing God's Kingdom, you will never lose focus. The enemy's efforts to distract you from your focus or discourage you with circumstances won't work. Race car drivers tell us the way they get through a tight line of cars and seldom hit anything is that they focus on where they want to go. They train themselves not to look at the wall or the cars they want to avoid but to focus on the open space they want to fill. That's what we need to do—focus on what we can do with God.

Too often we spend our energy on the things we would like to avoid rather than the things we want to accomplish. Paul explained that we do not look at things that are seen but at the things that are not seen.

> *When you set your affections on a big vision, you will never lose focus.*

A QUOTE ON SIGNIFICANCE

Don't let the word *significance* intimidate you. Don't let it stop you from pursuing a life that matters. When I talk about significance, I'm not talking about being famous. I'm not talking about getting rich. I'm not talking about being a huge celebrity or winning a Nobel Prize, or becoming the president of the United States. There's nothing wrong with any of those things, but you don't have to accomplish any of them to be significant. To be significant all you have to do is make a difference with others wherever you are, with whatever you have, day by day. No one stumbles upon significance.

We have to be intentional about making our lives matter. That calls for action—and not excuses. Most people don't know this, but it's easier to go from failure to success than from excuses to success. (John C. Maxwell, *The Power of Significance: How Purpose Changes Your Life*)

QUESTIONS TO CONSIDER

Do you have any areas of weakness that you have thought disqualified you from God using your life in a significant way? Will you dare to believe that He has chosen you, even in your weakness, to display His glory and power through your life?

Are there huge hurdles to climb in your life today? Consider Joshua looking at the great walled city and its mighty army. It was as if God told him, "See? Just march around seven times, blow the trumpets, and the wall will come down. Do you see that with me you have victory? Do you see it?"

Are you ready to upgrade your faith today to believe and see God do the impossible in and through your life?

> *"God has chosen the foolish things of the world to put to shame the wise, and God has chosen the weak things of the world to put to shame the things which are mighty; and the base things of the world and the things which are despised God has chosen, and the things which are not, to bring to nothing the things that are."*
>
> —1 CORINTHIANS 1:27–28

TRUTH THREE

Through the promises of God we connect to the power of God.

"You shall remember the Lord your God, for it is He who gives you power to get wealth, that He may establish His covenant."

—DEUTERONOMY 8:18

We are all alive in this amazing time for a reason. God continually reminds me that He is looking for people to partner with through His promises. As the world gets darker and darker, God is pouring out His glory and goodness on anyone with a loyal heart to be a blessing. In college I was not dreaming of how successful my business would be one day. I believed that God would use me one day to support the gospel in a big way.

God is so faithful when anyone gives cheerfully and willingly. He will pour out His blessings.

As I shared earlier, Scripture passages about God's heart to bless His people came alive to me over the next few months. Abraham, Isaac, Jacob, Joseph, Moses, Joshua, Daniel, David, and Solomon, just to name a few, were blessed so that they could be a blessing. God told them He would always be with them and accomplish His plans through them.

About 3 percent of Christians are in full-time ministry positions. Where does that leave the other 97 percent, and how do they fit into God's plans to advance His Kingdom? They are ministers too, and God wants to be involved in their occupations. Whatever your occupation or career is, you are a minister—because everybody has a calling to be a light in the darkness. Then as God blesses you, your tithes and offerings can help ministries accomplish what God wants them to do. His Kingdom is always advancing, and He is always looking to anoint anyone willing to finance His Kingdom. His favor and anointing are not dependent on your ability or skills; God looks at your heart—your willingness to sow into and bear fruit in His Kingdom.

In the book of Malachi is an amazing promise, actually a challenge from God, where He says to test Him: "Try Me now in this . . . if I will not open for you the windows of heaven and pour out for you such blessing that there will not be room enough to receive it, and I will rebuke the devourer for your sakes" (Malachi 3:10–11). Even in the first year of our business, when Pam and I were just getting started, we gave tithes and offerings willingly and generously, and God was more than faithful to pour out a blessing that was hard to contain.

> *Those who sow bountifully will also reap bountifully.*

A PROMISE BEING ESTABLISHED

From the beginning I was excited about partnering with God to finance the gospel. After encountering God in the meeting and my purpose in life dramatically changing, I spent a lot of time in Scripture getting a greater revelation of how God would partner with me. When God revealed to Jacob in an unusual dream how to peel strips exposing white on the rods and then placing them in the watering troughs, Jacob acted on this dream (Genesis 30:37–43; 31:10). The flocks conceived and bore offspring, greatly multiplying Jacob's flocks. I believed that God would anoint me in business and give me resources and strategies to be successful in the same way he blessed someone like Jacob.

It was close to the end of my junior year of college when a $5,000 check came in the mail from my Jewish grandfather. That was a lot of money in 1974. My grandfather had owned four successful women's apparel stores in Spokane for many years, but he had never done something like this before. I was fully convinced that God was partnering with me financially—that God had inspired my grandfather to send this money. The check was a confirmation from God that we were in business together and that He would give me the power to get wealth to establish His covenant (Deuteronomy 8:18). Somehow there was a deep confidence that God would be faithful to fulfill His promise.

Right away I wanted to fulfill my part of our partnership to establish His covenant.

I felt an urgency to act. I wanted to reveal to God that I was all in.

Filled with great excitement, I gave the entire check to our small church. It felt great to receive that money, but it felt even better to give it. My enthusiasm came from recognizing that God was bringing money my way so that it could flow through me, and this realization brought my faith to a new level. This was what I had been dreaming about. It didn't feel like a sacrifice. I wanted to give this money to our church. God was fulfilling His part of the plan so I could do my part. Our partnership had begun.

It's hard to explain how great I felt about God using me. His promise was being established in my heart. I could understand how excited Abraham must have been when Sarah became pregnant after waiting twenty-five years to fulfill God's promise of a child who would bless nations. It was a matter of faith. Without faith it is impossible to please God. He loves it when we begin acting on the truths of the Bible and the personal confirmations we get in our hearts—when we just *know* and when our responses are based on that inner knowing. It's like peace bubbles up inside and a joy flows within at the thought of doing what we have heard.

Suddenly the potential to start a business became a greater reality in my heart because I was developing an expectation of our partnership in business and a passion to support the gospel financially. I somehow knew God would give me a new idea or show me the kind of business that would be successful in the marketplace. I didn't know what it would be or how or when it would happen, so I continued reading in Scripture about giving, prosperity, riches, and financial promises. I started seeing God's heart toward His people, that He wanted to dwell among us and bless us so that we could then be a blessing to nations. I realized that the creator of this universe wants to live through His people so He can pour out His love to the world.

A few months after the exciting opportunity to give that check to our small church, a man named Tom Underhill asked me to work for him. He owned a store that sold unfinished furniture, so during the summer before my senior year of college, I worked for Tom as a warehouseman.

I had no idea that God was getting me involved in the type of business I would open six years later.

During my senior year, three months before I graduated from college as an occupational therapist, another check came from my grandfather.

This time it was $10,000.

I had not asked him for this, but I knew God had prompted him to give me this money, and since I was fully convinced that I was partnering with God to be a blessing, I joyfully gave this check away too. All I could do was rejoice at how faithful God was to fulfill His promises.

Now more than ever, I was convinced He would give me the idea, opportunity, and resources to start my business at the right time.

> *Without faith it is impossible*
> *to please God.*

IMPERFECT PEOPLE ACCOMPLISHING EXTRAORDINARY THINGS

Paul encouraged Christians to use the gifts given to them, one of which was a gift of giving (Romans 12:6–8). While I was still in college, I believed this gift was being birthed in my heart. I just knew I would not have to make this business happen or come up with my own idea. God and I were in this partnership together. At the right time He would tell me what business to start and then somehow provide the finances for it or show me what to do.

I knew I had very little to offer in this partnership compared to what God offered me. Success would happen not because of my plans or my ability to become successful. I was just willing to give this money away and wait to see what He would do. I was beginning to see what an amazing partner He was.

God gives us the power to get wealth and anoints us to be successful. I believed He had a purpose for my life and was showing me how much He desired to partner with me and provide resources to fulfill this plan.

In that season I learned that God continually reveals in Scripture how He provides more than enough for those who seek to do His will. He is looking for people who will rely on His strength and power and be loyal to walk with Him—people who will let His love and power flow into and through their lives. He wants His love to pour through us to those He puts before us on our journey through life with Him.

Regardless of occupation, we can minister to and serve people by being sensitive to their needs and letting God flow through our lives. God put on my heart that together we could make a difference by financing the gospel. As I started stepping toward my purpose, He came alongside me and partnered to help me realize my Kingdom purpose and destiny. When we give freely from our hearts, He pours so much more back into our lives. My life is an amazing testimony of His promise—that if we sow bountifully, we will also reap bountifully. When we give, it will be given back to us.

There are so many ways we can lay down our lives to serve people, and God wants to partner with us to do that in the ways He has called us. He wants to be right there beside us.

When you see Him begin stepping in as I did when finances started coming my way, you'll be as ecstatic as I was. You'll know that God is fulfilling His promise to give you the power to do all He has called you to in your Kingdom purpose. Imagine how Jacob felt when his flocks multiplied from a God-inspired dream about whittling sticks and putting them in watering troughs.

In my junior year of college I decided to always be a generous giver and to establish an ongoing lifestyle of giving in my heart. God chose me and had a plan for my life—to bear fruit and make a difference by living a life of significance. One moment I was living for my selfish needs, then out of His mercy He started redirecting my steps. He revealed that together we could make a difference and help a lot of people. He saw my heart and began directing my steps. I began experiencing His favor and grace on whatever I put my hands to.

The Bible is full of amazing stories of God redirecting people and then anointing them as they listened and obeyed, stepping out in faith into their destiny. But always remember that God uses imperfect people to accomplish extraordinary things. All He needs is a surrendered and willing heart. Then, when you willingly start stepping into your calling and purpose, He anoints you.

QUOTE ON PROMISES

If we can conceive of something in our hearts, it can be realized through experience. Promises are the engine room of possibility. When God gives us a promise, he releases us from logic to imagination. He wants us to see beyond the problem to its fulfillment. A promise takes us away from Egypt and moves us toward Canaan. A promise is a guaranteed outcome that empowers us to walk the steps toward freedom and realization. (Graham Cooke, *Radical Perceptions: Brilliant Thoughts for an Amazing Life*).

QUESTIONS TO CONSIDER

Are you willing to believe that God has precious promises for your life when you continually believe and trust that He will help you fulfill them?

Do you believe that God will keep His covenant to you and do His part, no matter the process or how long it takes, as you do your best to do your part? Will you listen and obey Him as it relates to your Kingdom purpose and calling?

Can you identify what kind of Kingdom partnership God is uniquely inviting you into?

"There is one who scatters, yet increases more; and there is one who withholds more than is right, but it leads to poverty. The generous soul will be made rich, and he who waters will also be watered himself."

—PROVERBS 11:24–25

TRUTH FOUR

God rewards those who diligently seek Him.

"Without faith, it is impossible to please Him, for he who comes to God must believe that He is, and that He is a rewarder of those who diligently seek Him."

—HEBREWS 11:6

God has a plan for our lives. Not just in business, but in every area of our lives. I saw this firsthand when God brought Pam into my life. Our church did a lot of fun social things together. Before we even started dating, I remember walking around with Pam at the World's Fair in Spokane, Washington, in 1974. It was a very special day.

As a junior in college preparing to graduate in a year, I was thinking a lot about my future and eventually marriage. A good friend encouraged me to ask the most beautiful and spiritual single lady in our church out on a date. Pam was three years older than me and already working as a teacher. I was pleasantly surprised when she said yes.

It took me only a handful of casual dates to totally fall in love. She was amazing. I could see right away she loved God and had a willing heart to serve Him. Pam was confident, outgoing, and full of life. Her eyes sparkled with joy. However, I would be lying if I did not say I was also smitten with her beauty. She was way out of my league. I was having a hard time studying because I was always thinking about her. I had never felt like that before and knew I had to do something about it, so I told her how I felt.

It was too much, too fast.

Pam confessed that she didn't have the same feelings for me at the time. She said she still wanted to spend time with me to see how things progressed. My heart wasn't prepared for that answer. I knew if I kept seeing Pam I would not be able to focus on my studies and my grades would tank. I also wasn't sure I could handle the possibility of her not falling in love with me. So I had a conversation with God and asked for His help in finding my future wife.

"God, you know I don't like this process of figuring out who I will marry one day," I admitted. "Whenever the time is right, please have my future wife fall in love with me and ask me out first. Then I can fall in love with her. Then I will know my emotions won't cause me to make the wrong decision."

As I prayed I knew how important this decision would be. I told the Lord I wanted His will for a wife, not mine. Just as I had with my finances and business, I decided I would simply trust Him and stop trying to figure it out. Since God had a plan for my life, I knew He would bring my future wife to me at the right time.

With this new plan in place, I began avoiding Pam. I didn't ask her out again because I didn't want to stir up my feelings. Looking back, I realize that I should have talked to her and told her why I couldn't spend time with her. But instead, we stopped talking, and following my lead, she also started avoiding me. Little did I know that she felt that I suddenly started acting as if she didn't exist without any explanation. Pam couldn't understand how a guy could confess his love for her one day and ignore her the next. Yet we both continued going to the same church meetings and growing in God.

About six months later some friends gathered at an ice cream shop to celebrate Pam's best friend's birthday. Five people were sitting at a booth for six people, and when Pam came in late and saw that there was only one seat left—next to me—she looked around, grabbed a chair from another table, and pulled up to the end of the booth. She wouldn't sit next to me. It was very awkward, but I deserved it.

Over the next year we were both very busy, me with school and Pam with work and helping with church things. Pam's dad had also been diagnosed with cancer, and she was visiting at home as much as possible.

In August before a three-month internship prior to graduation, I was at a church meeting where God showed up in an incredible way. This small church believed in all the spiritual gifts; I had heard prophetic words before, but I will never forget what happened in that meeting. The traveling pastor asked all the men to stand up and get in a line so his wife could give prophetic words to each of us individually. She was from out of town and did not know these men very well, yet she started to prophesy to them all, one at a time, poetically. I could quickly see God was speaking through her and "reading our mail" in poetry.

I was at the back of the line, so I had some time for a quick conversation with God.

Lord, I know you're going to tell me some great things, but can you confirm what I asked you about my wife? For her to make the first move so I can fall in love with her?

I was beginning to wonder if I had made a big mistake and would be single for the rest of my life.

Then the prophetic word came: "Oh, Mark, even in the dark, you are a spark unto the heathen so cruel;, but out of it you have come to be my jewel, so gentle, so persuasive, they could not resist thee. This shall be thy trademark thy whole life long, and in it you shall find thy being and go forth with a song. Oh, what a great delight that I have in thee. I shall lift thee up and bathe thee like the sea. I'll draw unto thee the woman that is right for thee, and then thou shall giggle in thy spirit and say tee-hee."

That day I got another glimpse of how much God loved me, cared about my future, and wanted to be involved in my life. I was rejoicing in my spirit, thanking God for hearing my prayers. Now I was willing to wait and trust that marriage would happen at the right time.

Pam was also present at that meeting in August. After hearing the promise that God would draw the right woman to me, she found herself wondering who that would be. She had been praying that God would bring the right man into her life as well. Later on she admitted to me that at one point God had challenged her with the question of whether she could accept the possibility of not marrying at all. Pam decided to lay marriage totally at God's feet and trust Him. She made sure to include that her desire was to marry and even included a list of qualities she desired in a man. She knew her Bible and knew that James 4:2 says, "You do not have because you do not ask."

A couple of months later I was surprised when Pam showed up at the door of the home I was living in during college. She had to drop something off, and to her dismay there I was, greeting her. She stepped in briefly, and we casually spoke. Then she left. A few moments later she knocked on the door again. When I saw her again, she shared some encouraging words that God had put on her heart to tell me.

"God is pleased with you and your faithfulness and wants you to know He is going to give you the desires of your heart," Pam said.

She could have easily ignored God's whisper to encourage me, but she didn't. Pam knew that when you feel a prompting of God's thoughts toward something or someone else and know that it should be shared, you quickly obey. Her attitude was more of a "*Really, God?*" thought as she rolled her eyes—but she obeyed.

She would later tell me how foolish she felt when she stepped back outside to leave and realized what she had said.

I had been the desire of his heart at one time, she thought with dismay. She was beginning to wonder what God was up to.

When Pam said I would get the desires of my heart, I immediately realized she wasn't aware that she still was the desire of my heart. But I also believed that God would draw the right woman toward me, so I determined to finish school and wait to see what God would do.

GOD IS FAITHFUL

God started fulfilling His promise four months later when Pam invited me to a potluck dinner. Christmas was approaching, and since she was a schoolteacher, Pam was available during Christmas break to organize activities for the singles during the holidays. When she called and invited me to a potluck dinner, I accepted, but after I hung up the phone, I told God the invitation didn't count.

She's calling a lot of people, not just me, I thought. She wasn't actually asking me out, so I wouldn't count the call as an official God-inspired invitation. Little did I know God had been working on Pam's heart. He had begun highlighting me to her in a new way. Her heart began softening, and she began forgiving me.

To my surprise, when I showed up at the dinner, Pam was waiting at the door for me and immediately started talking and asked if I was hungry. As she put food from each dish on her plate, she would also turn to me with a smile and ask if I wanted some. She was serving me, and I didn't know what to think. I was shocked. Then she went to an area across the room where we could have eaten together, but I didn't follow her. I was still avoiding her and went to the opposite side of the room. When she noticed where I was, she picked up her plate and came right over by me, and we spent the rest of the evening talking.

It was Christmas break for students, so Pam organized more events for everyone that week and invited me to each one. We spent a lot of time together. All my feelings for her began coming back. Then one evening after snow skiing together, as we were sitting by a beautiful fireplace, she asked me about my plans for the future. I quickly told her my dream.

"I'm going to make a lot of money in business to finance the gospel and help a lot of people," I said.

She had a glimmer in her eye and smiled. "That's great," she said. "I've always loved giving and look for ways I can be a blessing."

A few moments later she said she would like to invite me, our pastor, and his wife to dinner so I could tell them my plans. I was so excited that I didn't sleep that night. She had totally changed and had begun revealing her feelings toward me. She wanted to invite me to dinner with our pastor and his wife!

I was so glad she didn't ask me about my business plans that night—that is, how specifically I was going to make a lot of money. I had no idea what I would do or how it would happen, and I didn't know what I would tell our pastor. But I spent most of that night rejoicing in my spirit because of God's goodness. We were falling in love, and she seemed excited about my dream of giving a lot of money away.

The holidays were almost over, and everyone would soon return to school or work. I was driving to church and talking to God, telling Him I was in love with Pam and willing to make a lifelong commitment, and I asked Him to give me one more confirmation about her.

God, if she's supposed to be my wife, then please have her come and sit next to me in church.

Pam had never done that before, so I knew it would be a sign from God. As I walked inside the church, I noticed Pam sitting in the front row talking to some people, and my heart sank.

What had I done? Had I asked God for confirmation because I didn't have enough faith? I sat in the back row and the back corner, leaving room for one person next to me. In a few minutes Pam stopped talking to people and turned around to scope out the room. She spotted me, picked up her Bible and purse, and came back and sat right next to me! God is so faithful! He was demonstrating again that He wanted to co-labor with me in every area of my life, not just business.

Pam later revealed that she had been praying about taking the next step in our relationship. Before church she prayed about whether she should sit next to me that morning—because she wanted to. It was then that she heard God's still, small voice in her heart that if she did, she would be making a lifetime commitment to me. She did some soul-searching and decided she would.

God confirmed to both of us that it was His plan for us to get married and soon after, we were engaged. We were both excited because we knew that together, with God on our side, we could overcome anything that came our way.

A WILLING HEART

Jesus told us He would bless us if we seek God's will. Matthew 6:33 states, "Seek first the Kingdom of God and His righteousness, and all these things shall be added to you." Even the Lord's Prayer says, "Your Kingdom come. Your will be done" (Luke 11:2).

I trusted God for a wife in the same way I trusted Him to eventually establish me in a prosperous business. God rewards those who have faith in His plans and purposes. Our reward is knowing Him and His ways as His Son lives in us and through us. As with Moses, who asked God to reveal His ways and pleaded that He would go with His people, God saw our hearts to seek Him and our willingness to follow His ways. We each desired to do His will and marry someone with the same values and goals. Our priority in life was to advance His Kingdom, and God supernaturally put us together to fulfill His purposes for us. We were united and excited to work together. Both of us loved to give and wanted to finance the gospel in a big way to advance God's Kingdom. Together we were willing to make sacrifices to fulfill our dream.

Pam and I knew we would have some things to work through, but with our focus on our mission to advance His Kingdom and our willingness to work through life's issues, we've had an amazing marriage and journey together. We didn't do anything to earn God's favor. All we had to offer was willing hearts focused on His plans.

We've discovered together how faithful God is when we commit our hearts and future to Him, believing He will provide for our needs. He has not only prospered us in business—He has also blessed us spiritually, emotionally, and physically. All we had to do was say yes and trust Him to take whatever risk necessary to support His work. Looking back, we can see how He went before us and prepared the way for us to step into our destiny together. God has greatly rewarded us in love and abundant life!

Do you need to see God's reward in any aspect of your life? Perhaps that's because you haven't trusted or sought Him in that specific area. It's never too late to diligently seek His will!

> *God rewards those who have faith in His plans and His purposes.*

LAY EVERYTHING AT HIS FEET

Jesus taught us to pray for His Kingdom to come and His will to be done—to establish His Kingdom "on earth as it is in heaven." He came to do His Father's will. When you set your affections on God and His plans and purposes, God then sets His affections on you.

Jesus said, "Your heavenly Father knows that you need all these things. But seek first the Kingdom of God [His presence] and His righteousness [His will], and all these things will be added to you" (Matthew 6:32–33).

God had an amazing plan for my life, and He knew I needed to live from these Kingdom principles to do His will. I never thought about my business or dreamed about how big and successful it would be; my affections were on walking with God in relationship so that together we might advance His Kingdom and financially support ministries that were making a difference in the world. I prioritized getting out of debt so I could give generously whenever possible to fulfill God's purpose in my heart.

God looks at our hearts and motives, not at our ability or status. He is looking for people who want to do His will, who have united their plans and purposes with His. Whatever you are trying to accomplish, the odds of victory dramatically change when you are united with Him and He is on your side, directing your steps.

When the disciples wanted to know how to pray, Jesus told them to ask, "Your Kingdom come. Your will be done on earth as it is in heaven" (Matthew 6:10). It is God's will for us to live our best possible life, and Pam and I both wanted His will. That's why we kept asking for confirmations; we didn't just go by our feelings when making such a big decision about marriage—one of the most important decisions of our lives. We saw in each other a heart to serve God.

Pam and I have made mistakes. You could ask either of us, our employees, our daughters, or many others who could tell you about them. I had anger and control issues, among other things, that I needed to work on. But we both continually sought God's will, surrendered our faults to Him, and tried not to be conformed to or impacted by this world.

Over the years we've learned the importance of forgiveness, receiving the abundance of grace and His gift of righteousness through Jesus's blood to be transformed. We have prioritized laying our lives down before the Lord and asking for His will. We have committed our time and work to God, and He has been so faithful to bless what we have put our hands to.

When you lay everything at His feet and know that everything you have is given to you and belongs to Him, it is fairly easy to risk it all and start a business to support His work and do His will.

A QUOTE ON SEEKING HIM

I need to empty myself so that He can fill me. I need to say, "Here's my life, Lord. Let me wear the turban of your thoughts. Let you so fully possess me that even my mind is captured by you. . . . Take me. Fill me. Use me." In all the years that have followed, I have come back to the same realization over and again: I can't do anything for the Lord on my own. (Rolland and Heidi Baker, *Joyful Surrender: A 40-Day Journal to Greater Dependence on Jesus.* Heidi Baker and her husband, Rolland, founded Iris Ministries in 1980. Now Iris Global, their ministry includes Iris University, Bible schools, primary and secondary schools, medical clinics, farms, food and Bible distributions, churches, prayer houses, and more.)

QUESTIONS TO CONSIDER

Are you willing to lay everything at His feet and exchange your desires for your life and business for His? Give Him permission to accomplish His will in your life and in your business.

Do you desire and believe that God's will can be done through your life and business?

"Your Kingdom come. Your will be done."

—MATTHEW 6:10

TRUTH FIVE

Follow God with all your heart, and He will direct your steps.

"Trust in the Lord with all your heart, and lean not on your own understanding; In all your ways acknowledge Him, and He shall direct your paths."

—PROVERBS 3:5–6

In our first year of marriage Pam and I lived in a new apartment complex with a beautiful lake. I still remember the name of the apartments: "Sixty O One" (the address was 6001). Married life was great as we waited on God to show us what to do. Pam was already an elementary school teacher. I got a job as an occupational therapist at a hospital, and our first goal was to pay down our bills so we could be financially ready to start a business. I was filled with anticipation for God to show me what to do so we could get started.

We had signed a one-year lease, and if we wanted to stay, we needed to make another commitment for a second year before our lease was up because the complex was so popular. As I was contemplating renewing the lease, a thought popped into my head:

We should try buying a house.

This thought hadn't come earlier because we needed at least $1,000 to put down to qualify for financing, but we decided to start looking for a house anyway and see what God would do. While we looked, we moved to a different apartment that didn't require a one-year commitment.

The search for our first home centered around the Bellevue area east of Seattle because it would be convenient for Pam to get to work. We found an older three-bedroom house with a beautiful yard and a for-sale-by-owner sign. The price was $37,950. As we were looking at this home and I was thinking about the $1,000 I needed for a deposit, a new thought came to me. I could ask this owner to raise the price of the house by $1,000, and he could then stipulate that he would put $1,000 to go toward the deposit for financing—a win for both of us. He would get the original price he was asking, and we could qualify for the house. He agreed.

God anointed His idea that had popped into my head. We qualified for financing and bought the house in six weeks. One year later we sold that house for $52,950 and were ecstatic! God blessed us with $13,000 in one year simply from listening to His promptings.

With house prices rising quickly, we found a brand-new development with around fifty lots. They were just starting to build the first fourteen homes. We put $500 down on a $59,950 tri-level house that would be built in four months. The lot had a small stream and a treed greenbelt in the back, so other houses could not be built right behind us. We moved in with some friends temporarily while the house was being built. Again, we just knew that God was partnering with us financially and were so excited to see what God would do.

The $13,000 we made on the first house became a subject of prayer as I asked God for His wisdom on what to do with the money. We needed $4,000 to secure the financing at the closing of the new home after its completion. Of course, there were many ways to use the remainder—paying off some bills, buying a new car, or saving for our new business. But what came to my mind totally surprised me.

We can give all the money away.

After all, giving was the plan from the beginning.

Being recently married, I was focused on trying to be a good husband, so I knew that thought did not come from me. God was quietly reminding me of our partnership. He would give me the power to get wealth to establish His covenant with me. I would not recommend this as general advice to any newly married person, but in my situation I felt an amazing peace from God. I simply had to talk about it with my wife, who was excited about our new house.

It took me a week to get up the nerve to talk to Pam, but to my surprise she instantly agreed with the radical idea. No hesitation—we both wanted to give the money away. We were willing to start all over. We had done it once and knew God would continue anointing what we put our hands to.

Not only would this decision prevent us from buying the house, but it also meant a new car was out of the question. A week later Pam was on her way to work and passed a truck with a bunch of smashed cars going to the scrap pile. She sensed from the Holy Spirit a realization that cars just end up in the junkyard anyway. With a smile she rejoiced at God's wisdom as she released the desire for a new car. It was a very special God moment. We were living our purpose.

ANYTHING IS POSSIBLE

True faithfulness is placing God's Kingdom over our wants and needs. The story of Elijah and the widow is a wonderful illustration of that.

In 1 Kings 17:8–24 a widow and her son are in the middle of a long drought. She is so discouraged that she is out gathering sticks to make a fire so she can cook their last meal and die since she doesn't know where their next meal will come from. However, God tells Elijah to go to the woman. "See, I have commanded a widow there to provide for you," God says.

When Elijah sees this widow, he asks her to bring a little water in a cup. Now, in the middle of a drought, that is a big request, yet she immediately responds and turns to get the water. Elijah calls after her and asks her to bring him a morsel of bread too. She explains that she has only a handful of flour and just a bit of oil left for her and her son's last meal.

"Do not fear; go and do as you have said, but make me a small cake from it first, and bring it to me; and afterward make some for yourself and your son," Elijah says. "For thus says the Lord God of Israel: 'The bin of flour shall not be used up, nor shall the jar of oil run dry, until the day the Lord sends rain on the earth.'"

God fulfills His promises to multiply her flour and jar of oil as they are all able to eat for many days. Then her son becomes sick and dies. Having seen God multiply their food, the widow knows that anything is possible when you serve God and walk with Him. So she cries out to God and the prophet. And after Elijah stretches out on the child three times and prays, God revives her son!

This is a miraculous example of God's giving heart in partnership with people who have a giving heart.

When my wife and I decided to give away the rest of the money from the sale of our first house, we believed that this was part of our destiny. We were just excited to be part of His plan, and we had faith in God's love. We knew God would work out the details and help us overcome any obstacles in the future.

When God promises He will be with you, He is faithful to bless what you put your hand to. It is an easy decision to give freely what you've been given.

God is faithful. We can start over.

We gave the money away.

Six weeks later I received a phone call from a lady about the new house. She informed me that it would take two additional months to complete—now four months before it was finished. I didn't tell her I had given our deposit away and could no longer buy the house.

As I was hanging up, God prompted me. We still had four months. With God on our side, we could raise $4,000 to finance it. Pam's teaching job gave us access to a great credit union, so we qualified for a $2,500 loan on a car that was probably worth $1,000. Then we saved $500 and borrowed $1,000 from a relative.

God had this plan all along. We signed the paperwork four months later and moved all our possessions into our new house the next day. When I saw the sign in front of our development that day, I was blown away. It had changed. For months it had the picture of our tri-level for sale at $59,950, the price we agreed on the day before. Now it was selling for $73,000. In one day our equity on our brand-new home jumped up $13,000—exactly what we had given away!

God is so faithful. We were on an amazing journey together, and He was fulfilling His promise of abundant life. Three times He had provided money for us to support the gospel, and we still had the equity in our house to start a business. He was blessing us so we could be a blessing.

It's hard to explain how great that felt. In my heart I was rejoicing and thanking God for His faithfulness. My faith in His ability to partner with us rose to a new level. I knew He had led my steps through the entire process, and I was amazed at His faithfulness. We had found the greatest treasure, Jesus, who wanted to partner with us through life.

God's heart is to direct your steps and be a light to your path. He will always be there for you to help and strengthen you. He will never leave or forsake you when you believe and trust that Jesus is the way, the truth, and the life. Even in trials and storms, you can turn to Jesus for direction and comfort.

Believe and trust that God chose you, has a plan for your life, and will empower you to fulfill your purpose. He will always be there with you regardless of your circumstances. Even if you get a bad report, you can know that the creator of the universe—the one who gives life to the dead and calls those things that do not exist as though they do—is with you.

We live in a fallen world, and bad things do happen, but turning to Jesus and trusting Him will always give you the best results. Those who trust Jesus through testings will always come out stronger and better in their hearts and lives.

THE WORLD'S WAY OR GOD'S WAY

We live in an information age. The world is full of technology that gives solutions to problems and answers to questions almost before we can ask them. Just ask Alexa or Siri! But when it comes to major life decisions—choosing a mate, pursuing an occupation, or deciding what city to live in—you need a deeper soul search.

You have two choices. You can follow the world's way—what seems right to a man (see Proverbs 14:12)—and go with what feels best. Or you can weigh the facts, ask God to lead you, and then listen to what He says in His Word—to what He puts in your heart via that still, small voice in your head or that deep gut instinct.

God talks to us in many ways[1]. For over fifty years, whenever I've asked God for answers or direction, I've experienced a peace deep inside that has confirmed a solution I had been thinking about. I can't think of a time I have been disappointed by following His direction.

Give the Holy Spirit permission to show you ways that you may be leaning on your own understanding. Invite Him to teach you to trust Him in new ways with your whole heart.

> *Those who trust Jesus through a test will always come out stronger.*

TIME AND TIME AGAIN

Faith begins with a revelation of how much God loves and cares for you. He sent His Son, who demonstrated His love for people and gave His life to redeem us from death to life. Because Jesus laid down His life for us, we have a better covenant with better promises. As I was fully convinced in my heart that Jesus was my Lord, my provider, my protection, and my strength in every area of my life, I trusted that we were partners together in business.

---

[1] For more information on hearing God's voice, I recommend *4 Keys to Hearing God's Voice* by Mark and Patti Virkler.

God's plan from the beginning was to bless those who choose to follow Him, His people, so they would multiply in the city they live in. Deuteronomy 7:13 says, "He will love you and bless you and multiply you: He will also bless the fruit of your womb and the fruit of your land, your grain and your new wine and your oil, the increase of your cattle and the offspring of your flock, in the land of which He swore to your fathers to give you."

He was so faithful in fulfilling His promise to us. Time and time again, He came through for our business. I often had no idea what to do or which way to turn, but He would show up for us at every turn as wisdom. Just as God promised to be with Joshua as He had been with Moses, to give Joshua the promised land and never to leave or forsake him, He was always there for us—even when I was not strong or of good courage.

I must admit that as our company grew, I had to learn how to look to God and not at our circumstances. Over the years my trust in His faithfulness and ability to provide grew within me. He did not always come through the way I wanted or hoped for, but He always came through. Paul wrote that God is "able to do exceedingly abundantly above all that we ask or think, according to the power that works in us" (Ephesians 3:20). God took our company much further than I ever imagined.

> *Faith begins with a revelation of how much God loves and cares for you.*

Remember that God's plan from the beginning was to bless and multiply His people. That is why Jesus promises in Luke 6:38, "Give, and it will be given to you: good measure, pressed down, shaken together, and running over will be put into your bosom." Whatever you give out will be poured back into your life.

God can't lie. He is faithful and fulfills His promises. Jesus gave His life to give us a better covenant with better promises and access to His grace so He could live in us and through us here on earth.

A QUOTE ON TRUSTING

You must cultivate trust in your relationship with God, just like you do in any important relationship in your life. God's currency is trust, and the enemy's currency is fear, greed, or both. If you find your daily realities being more in the fear/greed category, then make the necessary adjustments. Trust isn't easy, but it's necessary. Sometimes you must stare down your fear—eyeball it face to face—and declare to it and to yourself that you trust God the Provider. God is not fragile, but our trust can be. One bad day for Wall Street and our confidence can come crashing down. (Johnny and Elizabeth Enlow, *Rise: A Reformer's Handbook for the Seven Mountains.* Johnny and Elizabeth are international speakers. Johnny is the author of *The Seven Mountain Prophecy: Unveiling the Coming Elijah Revolution.* The couple founded Restore 7 with trainings, blogs, and podcasts.)

QUESTIONS TO CONSIDER

Are you willing to acknowledge Him in every decision and anticipate how He will direct you?

Are there circumstances in your life or business that have caused you to waver in unbelief? God understands and is asking that you trust Him again—trust His ability to be faithful to His promises.

No matter what tests or trials come your way, will you trust that God will direct your steps and be faithful to fulfill His promises?

Don't waver in unbelief. Rather, be fully convinced that what God has promised He is able to do.

"He did not waver at the promise of God through unbelief, but was strengthened in faith, giving glory to God, and being fully convinced that what He had promised He was also able to perform."

—ROMANS 4:20–21

TRUTH SIX

Testimonies predict what Jesus can do in your life.

"The testimony of Jesus is the spirit of prophecy."

—REVELATION 19:10

As I was waiting on God for the business idea, I discovered that testimonies greatly encouraged and strengthened me. They established faith in my heart that God would fulfill His plans and purpose for my life. I knew God was no respecter of persons—that what He did for one He will do for another. Whenever a doubt began to creep into my mind, I would meditate on His promises and testimonies and surrender my heart to Him, asking for His will. I wanted the business He planned for me.

Reading about great Christians who started successful companies was very encouraging. So many different testimonies confirmed that from the beginning God's heart was to anoint and bless people in business—those who genuinely care for people and with integrity and honesty supply goods or services to the world He created and loves. I wanted the same blessing and fruitfulness for the business I started so I could then support and advance His plans and purposes in the world.

What He did for one He will do for another.

Testimonies throughout Scripture built my faith. I read how God was supernaturally involved with His people in their occupations and livelihoods to impact their spheres of influence. I knew that Jesus Christ is the same yesterday, today, and forever. So believing that God would be supernaturally involved with my business was not a stretch. Here are some highlights from the stories that inspired me to believe in a miracle God:

- God told Abraham, "I will make you a great nation; I will bless you and make your name great; and you shall be a blessing" (Genesis 12:2).
- Isaac obeyed the Lord, stayed in a foreign land during a famine, and had a hundredfold increase because the Lord blessed him (Genesis 26:1–13).
- Jacob made a deal with Laban for the speckled and spotted sheep, which were usually weaker, but God gave him a dream instructing how to peel sticks and put them in the watering troughs while the sheep were conceiving. Soon the stronger flocks were spotted and speckled and owned by Jacob (Genesis 30:27–31:13).
- Joseph had a dream about his brothers bowing down to him. His brothers did not like it, so they sold him as a slave. He ended up in prison, but that was all part of the plan. In prison he interpret-

ed a dream, then became Pharaoh's right-hand man and saved nations from a seven-year famine (Genesis 41:1–41).

- Bezalel was filled with God's Spirit in wisdom, understanding, knowledge, and all manner of workmanship to design artistic works with gold, silver, and bronze (Exodus 35:30–35).
- God spoke to Joshua about leading His people into the promised land and then emphatically promised He would be with him—that He would not leave or forsake him (Joshua 1:1–9). God promised, "No man shall be able to stand before you all the days of your life" (Joshua 1:5). So with God's help, Joshua led Israel into the promised land, defeating the giants and conquering mighty cities along the way.
- Finally, there is the famous story of David as a young boy. Knowing he was fighting in the name of the Lord, he slayed a giant and eventually became a great king (1 Samuel 17:29–53).

These Old Testament examples reveal the power of God partnering with those doing His will. The New Testament is also filled with supernatural testimonies of Jesus healing, restoring lives, and ministering to people's needs. In the first miracle in the New Testament Jesus turned six large jars of water into top-quality wine at a wedding. He also fed thousands of people with a few loaves of bread and fish. Then He told the disciples how to catch a multitude of fish after fishing all night without catching anything. God poured out His creative and restorative power throughout the Bible to reveal His goodness in the marketplace.

THE POTENTIAL FOR MIRACLES

There are many examples of people empowered by God in business over the past two hundred years that have inspired me. Throughout my life these testimonies inspired me to partner with God. These men include J. C. Penney, founder of department stores; R. G. LeTourneau, manufacturer of earthmovers and other heavy equipment; James I. Kraft of Kraft foods; William Colgate, founder of Colgate; George Washington Carver, an agricultural scientist who came up with around three hundred ways to use peanuts; and Gunnar Olson, owner of a Swedish plastics company, who also founded the International Christian Chamber of Commerce and has been a president of the Full Gospel Businessmen's Fellowship. The testimonies of these men—how God inspired them in different ways and blessed them so they could be a blessing—stirred my heart.

One story that has blessed and encouraged me was that of Matt McPherson, who started Mathews, Inc., now the largest archery manufacturing company in the world. As a young man ministering the gospel through music and leading worship, he realized how hard it would be to support his family. Then God gave Him an amazing promise to prosper him in business so he could be self-sufficient in ministry.

Matt had no desire for fame or power; he simply wanted to make a difference. A few years later God spoke to Him again: "I know every answer to every problem in the world. If men only asked me, I would give them the answers." Matt was overwhelmed by this promise. He dropped to his knees and cried out to God about the things that concerned him.

Growing up with a hobby of making and shooting bows, Matt asked God how to build a better bow. Several weeks later, at 3 a.m. he woke up seeing a piece of paper suspended before his eyes. On it was a sketch of a new concept for a compound bow. God gave him an initial concept for what would eventually launch the Mathews Archery Company, which would change the archery industry forever.[1]

Rarely will a new idea come that way, but God is always faithful to fulfill His promises. Today Matt owns at least twenty patents, with more pending. He and his wife have given themselves completely to God for His glory, are very generous givers, and can carry out their music ministry with great liberty.

Faith in a testimony or a promise of God connects us to His power and opens the door for Him to move for and through us. The more I believed in the testimonies of other businesses, the potential for miracles to happen in my business increased.

Another of my favorite stories is about the miracle that happened to Gunnar Olson, owner of a Swedish plastics company. Pallets containing huge plastic bags for covering hay were ready to be shipped, but it was discovered that the bags were ruined—sealed shut, impossible to salvage. The loss of this shipment would have put Gunnar out of business. So he and his family prayed in faith and commanded molecules to migrate back to where they had been. Then they laid hands on all the pallets, and the bags were supernaturally restored. This testimony went all around Europe and encouraged businesspeople around the world.

Donny Godsey, the owner of a video company, saw a clip of this testimony. So when his business encountered a similar situation, he asked God to repeat the miracle. Four tapes of raw digital footage from two

---

[1]Bill Johnson, *Dreaming with God: Secrets to Redesigning Your World through God's Creative Flow* (Shippensburg, PA: Destiny Image Publishers, 2016), 117–19.

events shot a weekend earlier had come out ruined—a garbled mess with little or no audio—which could have wrecked the reputation of his small business. He, his family, and his video editor got together and prayed that God would alter the tapes, and when they finished praying, Donny had a strange sense of peace that God would answer. They put a tape in and saw it clear up right before their eyes, with full sound. The other tapes were still damaged, but over the next day as they kept believing, those tapes cleared up too. This miraculous answer saved Donny's business and also ministered to his family when they needed a reminder of God's love and care for them.[2]

Through this testimony I saw how intimately God wants to be involved with our businesses and families. It taught me not to look at negative circumstances but to turn to God and believe in His goodness. He cares about every aspect of our lives.

FITTING INTO GOD'S MASTER PLAN

Abraham, the father of faith, believed God "gives life to the dead and calls those things which do not exist as though they did" (Romans 4:17). He did not waver at the promise of God but was fully convinced that what He promised He was able to do (Romans 4:20–21).

Another amazing testimony that increased my faith for miracles in business came from Bill Johnson in his book *Dreaming with God*. Boys from a homeless shelter in southern California, boys without a good education, tapped into God's creative nature and developed twelve patents that have

---

[2] Adapted from Os Hillman, *The 9 to 5 Window: How Faith Can Transform the Workplace* (Ventura, CA: Regal Books/Gospel Light, 2005), 138–39.

captured the attention of major toy-makers and manufacturers around the country. One of the toys produced is an anti-gravity hovercraft flying machine. When first approached about this idea, one expert told them a hovercraft would be aerodynamically impossible to fly. So the boys went to prayer, and God gave them a vision showing them how to make it, what materials to use, and how it would fly. It was up and flying within two days. At the time Bill Johnson wrote about this, they had over fifty household inventions and attributed their success to three things:

1. They believed they lived under an open heaven.
2. They believed they had dominion over this world—over the economy and the technologies of this earth.
3. They prayed in the Spirit for up to three hours a day. They believed that when they prayed in tongues, they tapped into Holy Spirit's creative nature.

These boys were poorly educated and could have been considered society's throwaways, but they brought solutions to everyday problems and challenges. What an example of God flowing into and through His people! He loves to take the weak and make them strong.

I hope these testimonies stir your faith to believe that God will give you solutions to problems. He is no respecter of persons. Again, what He does for one He will do for another.

Jesus gave His life to set us free so we could live with Him on this amazing journey to advance His Kingdom. Revelation 12:11 tells us, "They overcame him by the blood of the Lamb and by the word of their testimony, and they did not love their lives to the death." All of these business-related testimonies helped me remember how I fit into God's master plan to fill the earth with His glory and goodness, and they stirred up my anticipation and expectation that He would always be with me.

The testimony of Jesus predicts what God can do in and through your life. Testimonies reveal what God has done in co-laboring with His people. His goodness flows through people's testimonies and activates our expectancy. When we remember and confess testimonies, our faith in God's power and ability to fulfill His promises grows. They will strengthen our belief in God's willingness to flow through us.

We serve a miracle God who calls things into existence that do not exist and who can create solutions to any problem. When we partner with God, all things are possible.

The greatest testimony is that Jesus was crucified and resurrected to bring us abundant life. That's our inheritance in Christ; He lives in and through us. You can step into that inheritance when you remember what God has done and believe He can do it for you too.

That was King David's experience. He wrote, "Your testimonies I have taken as a heritage forever" (Psalm 119:111). He continually remembered what God had done for him and rejoiced that God would continue blessing and protecting him.

Psalms 23 and 103 are great examples of David's testimony of what God had done and would do for him. The enemy wants us to forget what God has done and lose faith in what God will do, so he tries to distract us with bad news and discourage us with our circumstances. But we can overcome with the word of our testimony (Revelation 12:11). I've won many battles that way.

When we partner with God, all things are possible.

I believe Paul overcame by the word of this testimony—"I have been crucified with Christ; it is no longer I who live, but Christ lives in me; and the life which I now live in the flesh I live by faith in the Son of God, who loved me and gave Himself for me" (Galatians 2:20). Jesus urged His disciples to remember the testimony of how He fed five thousand people with five loaves of bread and fish (Mark 6:38–44) and then four thousand with seven loaves of bread and a few fish (Mark 8:5–9). He was essentially asking them, "Can't you see what we can do together? Open your heart and believe that all things are possible with God!"

Every testimony you hear opens the realm of possibility to do the impossible.

ALL THINGS ARE POSSIBLE

Jesus said He could do nothing on His own, only what He saw the Father doing (John 5:19). In other words, He did all His miracles with the Father, not by Himself. And about a third of them were marketplace miracles.

God wants to work with us in our businesses to accomplish great things. So why would He not do that with you? And why not now?

You may not feel very strong or powerful, but with God you are. God sent an angel to Gideon to remind him of that fact—that despite the discouraging circumstances Gideon saw all around him, he was a mighty man. And one of the reasons Gideon was mighty was that he remembered the testimonies of what God had done. He had heard how God delivered Israel from Egypt many years before (Judges 6:11–14). He needed a little convincing, but God promised to be with him in defeating the oppressive Midianites. And Gideon believed—he was all in. With God, he wasn't afraid to go into battle with just three hundred men against a much larger army. All he needed was confirmation from God that they were in it together.

God is confirming the same thing for you. He is with you in your work. And with Him all things are possible. Will you choose to focus on your circumstances and challenges? Or will you remember all the times God has performed miracles throughout Scripture and expect Him to do the same for you as you partner with Him in advancing His Kingdom?

We need to purpose in our hearts to remember what God has done with other businesses and in our businesses. We can and should be inspired by the testimony of His faithfulness and love. We should never forget what He has done for us and many others. We don't want to be like Israel, who sometimes forgot the miracles God had done in delivering them from bondage in Egypt. Whenever they forgot His power, they ended up helpless, oppressed, or even captive. Always remember, believe in and meditate on His promises and testimonies.

Remembering what God has done strengthens your resolve to walk with Him and to know He is with you in all circumstances. This is not the message you will get from the enemy. He wants you to think God has left you. He wants you to lose faith in God's promises and forget all the good God has done and will continue doing.

As our company grew over the years, I learned to live with expectancy. I developed the expectation that God would show up and help solve our multitude of problems by giving us ideas, solutions, and Kingdom resources. Much of this expectation came from testimonies—those I had read or heard about, as well as our own experiences with God.

A QUOTE ON THE POWER OF TESTIMONIES

Testimonies are the résumé of God. What He has done in the past, He will do again. What He has done for someone else, He can do for you. Testimonies are a key that opens a door for us to go after more. They are the key for us to win (see Revelation 12:11) and the prophecy of what God will do again (see Revelation 19:10). . . . I encourage you to make testimonies personal by remembering them, praying them over your life, and then spreading your own testimonies as God shows up on your behalf. (Andy Mason, *God with You at Work.* Andy is the director of "Heaven in Business," a global online learning community at *Heaveninbusiness.com.*)

QUESTIONS TO CONSIDER

Testimonies tell us what God has done and what He is willing to do now and in the future. Will you purpose to move forward and cling to the testimonies of Scripture and people who have experienced God's miraculous power and provision? Will you commit to establishing them in your heart and expect them to become your testimonies too?

> *"I remember the days of old; I meditate on all Your works; I muse on the work of Your hands. I spread out my hands to You; my soul longs for You like a thirsty land."*
>
> —PSALM 143:5–6

TRUTH SEVEN

God will answer us when we ask for His grace and favor for our assignment.

"Your word is a lamp to my feet and a light to my path."
—PSALM 119:105

Sometimes when we pray for guidance and direction from God, we don't immediately hear from Him. All we can do is wait, be patient, and have faith that His timing is perfect.

While working on various jobs, I spent a lot of "carpet time" on my knees, asking God to reveal what type of business I should start. I didn't hear anything specific for three years, so all I could do was work hard and commit my work as unto the Lord. I both believed in Him and expected direction from Him.

After working as an occupational therapist for the first year, I decided to sell life insurance. This choice turned into a disaster. Every day I came home knowing it wasn't the job I wanted. All the job tests I took said the same thing—that when I found something I had confidence in, I could sell it. I had no confidence selling whole life insurance and quickly knew it was not a way to earn a living.

After three months I received a call from Tom Underhill, a friend from our small church whom I had worked for the summer before my senior year of college. He had just bought the store of unfinished furniture from his father and after letting a full-time employee go, he wanted me to work for him. Having run out of potential insurance customers and realizing I was not gifted for cold calling, I quickly accepted.

Little did I know how monumental this job change would be. I still knew I would start a business one day, but I didn't know when, how, or what kind of business it would be. All I could do was continue building and strengthening my faith to hear and follow God. I didn't want my faith to waver. I needed to hold on to God's plans and purposes for my life—to live by faith, to always have an expectancy about my business and His partnership in it.

Scripture tells us that "faith comes by hearing, and hearing by the word of God" (Romans 10:17). So I kept reading biblical testimonies of people who found themselves in impossible situations and relied on God to get them through—stories like Moses and the exodus, David and Goliath, and Daniel in Babylon. I kept these in my mind, but more importantly, I established them in my heart. That is how faith works. First we acknowledge in our minds God's will and direction. Then, as this revelation is rooted in our hearts and we become fully convinced, we take steps toward obeying. Faith is activated when we hear His words in our hearts and then take confident steps toward their fulfillment.

During that season Jesus asked a challenging question: "When the Son of Man comes, will He really find faith on the earth?" (Luke 18:8). That question implies that many would not believe what Jesus did for them on the cross or that He would work in their lives. If I wanted to make a difference in life and help build His Kingdom, I knew I had to develop strong faith in Him and what His resurrection had accomplished for me. Businesses fail every day. I didn't want mine to be one of them.

The most important business-related decision I faced was what kind to start. So I waited and continued believing that God would show me in His time. I didn't want to put any limitations on Him. I wanted His will because it is always the most rewarding.

> *Faith is activated when we hear His words in our hearts and then take confident steps toward their fulfillument.*

A NUDGE FROM GOD

When I started working at Underhill's Unfinished Furniture store, I began in the warehouse. But it wasn't long before I was selling. Within a year I became a manager at one of his stores. I enjoyed sales and the challenges that came with it—increasing sales and improving the store. At the time the unfinished furniture business was growing in popularity because solid oak was in demand and very easy to finish.

Oak tables were beautiful with a walnut oil finish and were easy to repair if scratched. We could demonstrate the ease of finishing, emphasize the quality, and help people see how much they saved. It was very rewarding to help people find a high-quality piece of furniture that they would enjoy for a long time at a great price.

I enjoyed the challenge of managing a store and trying to close every sale. I was confident and worked well with the customers. I remember one month helping close a high percentage of the sales—it was the best month the store had ever had. I could feel God's blessing on what I was putting my hands to.

Pam and I sometimes drove to Spokane to visit my family, especially around the holidays. Once when we were there I visited Spokane's only unfinished furniture store and realized they did not carry the solid oak lines we were selling so well in Seattle. Suddenly I just knew I should open an unfinished furniture store in Spokane. This was going to be my new business.

It wasn't that I received a dramatic confirmation. I just had an amazing excitement and confidence that God would partner with me to run this business so that I could help advance His Kingdom.

According to Mark and Patti Virkler in their book *4 Keys to Hearing God's Voice*, His voice sounds like spontaneous thoughts that light up your mind.[1] I have found that when something pops into my mind, it's probably a nudge from God, especially when it brings peace and I know it lines up with His Word and what He has been telling me.

So I didn't hesitate. We returned to Seattle, put our house on the market, and started planning to move to Spokane, find a location, and open a store. We made another radical step of obedience.

Our house sold for about $87,000, so we had $25,000 after closing costs to start our business. As the moving time approached, I realized I needed to research the responsibilities of owning a business. Even though

---

[1]Mark and Patty Virkler, *4 Keys to Hearing God's Voice* (Shippensburg, PA: Destiny Image Publishers, 2010).

I had a little experience managing a store for a year and a half, there were many things I hadn't been involved with, like accounting, taxes, payroll, and buying and keeping the right amount of products in stock. Then there were financial statements, legal issues and government regulations, employee issues, and the financial responsibility of keeping the expenses lower than the income. Fortunately, I wasn't going to be starting a business on my own. God and I were in it together. So I set out to get some answers.

My Jewish grandfather who lived in Spokane had owned four successful women's apparel stores for many years. So I asked him for advice. I explained what I was doing, told him I had sold our house in Seattle, was committed to opening a Spokane store, and then highlighted many of the unknowns.

"You're not ready," he said with a stern face. "You need at least three to four more years of experience. You will fail."

I wasn't prepared for that response. I couldn't tell Him I was partnering with God and that God had all the experience and solutions I needed.

Without thinking, I said, "If that's what I need, then I could ask Tom Underhill to partner with me. I worked for him in Seattle, and he opened a store in Spokane that he eventually sold because it was hard to find someone to run it. I'm sure he would be interested."

That hadn't been my plan at all. It was another example of a spontaneous thought from God that popped into my head, if only to address my grandfather's initial concerns about my lack of experience. Underhill had been in business a long time in Seattle. I told my grandfather I would open a store in two or three months. I was frustrated that he was unwilling to advise, but I wasn't discouraged.

Two days later my grandfather called and asked me to come back to see him because he had some ideas that could help me. When I arrived he told me a story I had never heard.

"Did you know my first real job was selling ladies' shoes?" he asked. "Like you, I was a great salesman. I helped that store become very successful. So one day one of my uncles came to me with a proposal: 'I'll give you $10,000 to set my son up in a shoe business.' My uncle wanted me to be a business partner with him. All I had to do was teach his son the business."

"What'd you do?" I asked my grandfather.

"I agreed. And in just over three years, business was booming. We were growing so fast that it needed to expand. My uncle came back to me with another offer. This time he wanted to buy my half of the business for $10,000 since his son now understood how to run it. I didn't have an agreement with my uncle on how to value the business, but I knew that figure was far too low. I told my uncle, 'No way.' The business was worth much more than that."

"Did he go higher?" I asked my grandfather.

My grandfather shook his head. "No. He said, 'Take this offer or I'll pull my money out of the business and you won't be able to pay your bills.'"

My grandfather knew he had no choice. He had spent three years of his life starting a business from which he had to walk away.

"You will never partner with Tom Underhill," my grandfather said resolutely. "I will help you."

He gave me the name of a great retail accountant to help answer a lot of my initial questions and offered to help me look for a location. God had turned everything around. My grandfather bought our first location, complete with room to expand, because we knew we would eventually need more retail space. A third of the upstairs was available, and there was a basement for storage. My grandfather became my landlord and even offered a $10,000 loan so I could have enough inventory to open this store.

That was God! He set it all up. I could not have planned it any better. It isn't easy to explain, but as soon as I committed to opening a store that would help finance the Kingdom, I felt God's involvement with every aspect of this business—especially the timing.

IMPERFECT AND UNLIKELY PEOPLE

God is always speaking, and His desire is for you to prosper and be in health. He is always knocking at the door of your heart because He wants to be involved in your life. He is always available and looking to pour His favor and grace into people's lives to advance His Kingdom. Grace and favor are not dependent on your ability and cannot be earned. Grace is His empowerment to do what you could not normally do. They both come with the assignment God gives you.

We receive God's grace and favor by faith as we step into our assignment. Obedience to God's direction brings favor. I'm so thankful that He uses imperfect and unlikely people to accomplish extraordinary things. We moved to Spokane to open a store, and God gave us great favor as doors opened. He gave us favor with my grandfather; I was simply looking for advice and got so much more. We also quickly found an amazing location on the best retail street in town, and it even had a basement for storage and also an elevator. God gave us favor by setting us up just before the owner of our competitor retired. I was beginning to see what an amazing partner and provider Jesus would be.

We receive God's grace and favor by faith as we step into our assignment.

I didn't understand God's timing at first, but as I looked back, I could see that He had been clearly preparing the way for my business for years. The popular lines of unfinished, solid oak furniture were available, so we had a great product to advertise at a very competitive price. I'm pretty sure we were the smallest furniture store ever to open in Spokane—just two thousand square feet of retail space—yet God blessed us. We made money our first year. We expanded and opened more stores as opportunities continued coming our way. I knew I was fulfilling His will and was excited to be on this journey with Him.

I encourage you on your faith journey to acknowledge that without His grace and favor for the assignment, you can't truly succeed. Remind Him today that you are aware of your need for Him and then by faith trust that His help is available for exactly what is required for you and your business to be a blessing for His Kingdom.

Grace and favor are core values dependent on knowing how much God cares about every detail of your life, the important decisions you make, and the path you will take. Because I knew He cared about me and all aspects of my life, I believed He would direct my steps, put His thoughts and ideas in my mind, and prompt me in certain directions by His peace. I believed God already knew the best direction for me; all I had to do was lean in and listen.

Trusting His direction and will for our life gave Pam and me a huge advantage in business and life as we listened for and followed His leading.. Most businesses pay a lot of money for expert advice on how to succeed. I spent quiet time in the morning to connect with God and listen carefully—to incline my ear to Him. At times He led me to seek expert legal or financial advice, but I looked to Him first. His directions continually blessed me and gave me amazing opportunities in business.

Jesus always demonstrated God's provision. He told Peter to launch out into the deep and let down his nets for a catch. Peter had the right attitude and level of expectancy: "Master, we have toiled all night and caught nothing; nevertheless at Your word I will let down the net" (Luke 5:5). Then they caught so many fish the nets started breaking. God provided more than enough, and the multitudes saw and were astonished.

When God prompts us to do something, it's our choice whether to step into His direction. When He flashed into my mind the realization that Spokane needed an unfinished furniture store and the timing was right, I took steps to make it happen. It's hard to describe, but because of the peace and excitement in my heart, I just knew it would be successful. I knew God would provide.

A QUOTE ON HEARING AND BELIEVING

Repair and restoration are now. "In the time of my favor, I will answer you, and in the day of salvation, I will help you" (Isaiah 49:8).

In 2 Corinthians 6:2, after referring to this promise from Isaiah, Paul wrote, "I tell you now is the time of God's favor, now is the day of salvation." These promises are in the now for everyone who will perceive them and receive them by faith.

Are you wondering what happened to your now? Stay in tune with the promise. Don't just live toward it—live from it. Act like you already have it, even if you don't see proof that it is real. Breakthrough doesn't come when you get the job, the spouse, or the financial means you have been praying to receive. Breakthrough happens the moment you believe. (Bob Hazlett, *Think like Heaven: Change Your Thinking, Change Your World.* Scripture quotes are from the NIV. Bob is a friend to leaders and a sought-after speaker and author.)

QUESTIONS TO CONSIDER

Do you believe God cares about every aspect of your life and business?

Do you recognize that because He cares, He has the better ways and plans for the practical steps you need to take and that He's willing to share them with you as you learn to lean in and listen for His directions?

Commit today to consistently make time to hear His input as you make important decisions.

"To him [the shepherd] the doorkeeper opens, and the sheep hear his voice; and he calls his own sheep by name and leads them out."

—JOHN 10:3

TRUTH EIGHT

God will always answer those with expectant hearts.

"My sheep hear My voice, and I know them, and they follow Me."
—JOHN 10:27

A belief that God will do amazing things doesn't always include an instruction book. My faith was growing, and my business idea was taking shape, but my heart was still filled with so many questions—a chorus of *who, what, where, when, why,* and *how* crammed inside my head.

When should I open?

What was God's timing?—not only for starting the business but also for when I should expand it—when I should hire more help, make improvements, or grow the warehouse. I didn't want to get ahead of His plan. So I kept trying to make sure we were in step. I wanted to trust His promptings completely.

How will I make the best decisions for the business?

To answer that question, I needed to establish a time and place to continually connect with God so I could listen and follow His direction.

Making time to seek God heightened my expectation of hearing Him so we would overcome any obstacles that came our way—together.

Where is the best location to open a furniture store?

Wherever God guided me, I was determined to follow His voice, promptings, and leading.

Why am I taking this risk?

I didn't earn or deserve His partnership, yet Jesus gave His life to "purify for Himself His own special people, zealous for good works" (Titus 2:14).

What is my responsibility to my employees and my community?

This was going to be an amazing journey. There would probably be competition, struggles, and setbacks. But I knew we would win many victories and help many people, not only by releasing the gospel around the world but also by blessing those working for my customers and me.

I felt as though by faith I had stepped out of the boat and into the water to open a store. And it felt as though I had to make hundreds of critical decisions quickly. How much rent could I afford? How big should the sign be? How much and when should I advertise? What products should I stock? How could I know what would consistently sell? How should I price the product, and how much should I spend on displays? How much help would I need? Who should I hire, and how much should I pay them? How would I keep track of everything and pay all the bills? I had to learn how to make good decisions with God's help, which needed to happen quickly.

God waits for us to sit at His feet and receive His answers. My relationship with the King of kings, my partnership with Him, was my greatest treasure. Because I'm a morning person, that's when we met. But it always looked different. My biggest struggle was taking the time to listen and connect with Him through His Word and prayer because my mind would always drift toward business and the decisions I needed to make.

God had already shown me what an amazing provider He is. He had arranged for two big checks to be sent to me in college. He had given me strategies to buy two houses, even when circumstances did not seem favorable. He had given me a beautiful wife who loved Him and was 100-percent committed to advancing His Kingdom. And He had turned my grandfather's heart toward helping me, giving much-needed advice and arranging my first location on one of the busiest streets in Spokane. I knew God had answers to all my questions and that He wanted to be involved in all the decisions. All I had to do was take the time to pause with expectation and ask for His direction and guidance and search His word for clues.

GOD'S TIMING

The store opening was set for June 1, 1980. But nothing I could do would set up my success.

God sets up our success.

Looking back, I can see how God influenced when we should open. Originally I wanted to open on May 1 and then advertise some on Memorial Day weekend. So I started getting the store ready for a grand opening. It was an exciting time of planning and preparing, which included displaying the furniture, prepping and pricing it, and adding accessories. We finished some samples of unfinished oak to show what they would look like. An office was set up to keep track of sales and inventory, and a couple of students were hired to work part-time during afternoons. Signs were made describing our layaway and delivery policies. Fortunately, some of the furniture I ordered for our store opening did not arrive in time, so our opening date was moved back to June 1.

On May 18 Pam and I were at a lake north of Spokane when we heard the news: Mount St. Helens had erupted on the west side of Washington State over three hundred miles from Spokane. The most destructive volcanic event in our country's history, it destroyed over two hundred fifty homes. The authorities recommended everyone go home. So despite a clear blue sky above us in Spokane, we followed their instructions and headed back home.

We left a little before 3 p.m., and on our way it began snowing ash from an ever-growing and darkening cloud. By the time we had reached home at 3:30, it was as dark as night. It was eerie and unusual. The city was covered in a ghostly ash from the blast. It looked as if it were the end of the world. In the following days city residents were advised to avoid driving and were asked to stay inside. If we had to go out, we were encouraged to wear masks so as not to breathe in the ash, which was basically a mixture of rock, mineral, and glass particles. Strong winds carried the ash as far east as Oklahoma and Minnesota![1]

For a while, stores shut down as Washington coped with the aftermath of the blast and began the long process of cleaning up the three to four inches of ash on the streets. This event affected many businesses with no customers for several weeks. But it just gave us more time to get ready because we pushed our grand opening to June 1. Had we opened before May 18, it could have been devastating to our new business.

---

[1] https://www.thereflector.com/stories/scenes-from-mount-st-helens-a-week-after-the-aftermath, 294538

This meant there was a pent-up demand for business when we opened. Much as in the lockdown during COVID, those in the market to buy furniture couldn't go out and look in stores since they were closed. Therefore, when we finally opened our doors, there was a real demand. This led to our having a great first month of sales.

In our case, God prevented a disaster from impacting our stores opening.

Another blessing came one month after we opened when the other unfinished furniture store in town closed and went out of business. The owner was ready to retire, and he advertised a big going-out-of-business sale that brought a lot of people into his store. Many of the people who came were looking for solid oak pieces to complete the sets they had bought in Seattle and Portland. His five pieces of solid oak sold quickly. After that, he told everyone about the new store that had a lot of solid oak. I had no idea that would happen, but it certainly influenced the success of our first year of business.

These two unexpected events had impacted our opening. As I said, God sets us up for success.

DIRECTING MY STEPS

I had read that 90 percent of startup businesses fail in the first five years and that very few are successful on a second try. So I needed to know that God was with me each step of the way. I held onto one promise above all others: that God and I were in this together.

I found a lot of encouragement in the first chapter of Joshua as I established God's promises in my heart. God told Joshua to lead His people into the land He had promised and to possess it:

> "As I was with Moses, so I will be with you. I will not leave you nor forsake you. Be strong and of good courage, for to this people you shall divide as an inheritance the land which I swore to their fathers to give them. Only be strong and very courageous, that you may observe to do according to all the law which Moses My servant commanded you; do not turn from it to the right hand or to the left, that you may prosper wherever you go. This Book of the Law shall not depart from your mouth, but you shall meditate in it day and night, that you may observe to do according to all that is written in it. For then you will make your way prosperous, and then you will have good success. Have I not commanded you? Be strong and of good courage; do not be afraid, nor be dismayed, for the Lord your God is with you wherever you go." (Joshua 1:5–9)

God promised that He would be with me—that we were business partners. I determined to spend time listening for His voice, receiving direction, and co-laboring with Him as well as I could. I surrendered my expectations—not my faith or anticipation but any specific agenda—because I knew not everything would go as planned.

This passage in Joshua became a life-giving promise that God would always be with me, no matter the circumstances—that He would never leave or forsake me, even if I made mistakes, took a wrong turn, or did something in my strength rather than in His. For a Type-A personality like me, it's hard to stop moving—I got to work at 6:30 in the morning, doing the books and receiving inventory before the store opened at 10:00, sold all day, and then loaded up our van and delivered furniture, sometimes until 8 or 9. I was intense and passionate about getting things done, always moving quickly to keep up with everything. So the time sitting with Him in the morning was important.

My main sources for learning were the Bible, books, and church services. There are so many books on how to hear God's voice, but I didn't know of any at that point in my life. The Scripture that helped me make decisions was Proverbs 3:5–6: "Trust in the Lord with all your heart, and lean not on your own understanding; in all your ways acknowledge Him, and He shall direct your paths."

I tried to trust Him with all my decisions, always acknowledging His wisdom and not assuming I would have the solutions. In other words, I would not depend on my limited knowledge or the world's strategies for being successful. I would keep turning to His wisdom and guidance with an open heart.

God's guidance can come from many directions. I tried to be aware of new thoughts, impressions, or unusual ideas that popped into my head and highlighted important issues. Often during a church service the minister would say something that directly applied to our business. The important thing was to keep looking and listening for God; He would find ways to make His will known to me. As a result, I continually leaned into God for direction and received His wisdom and guidance.

When we step out of the boat and onto the water in faith, the first step doesn't always make sense or align with expectations for getting a desired outcome. That's because God gets the glory. When He intervenes to do the improbable and the impossible, we can know the results belong to Him.

That's how it felt when we opened the store. As stated earlier, His direction led us to a space that was only two thousand square feet. You can sell only what you can display; catalog sales were hard then. The stores I had worked for in Seattle were at least five times as large, but God gave me real peace about opening in that small location. My business did not threaten other furniture stores, and even though it seemed like a big risk, looking back, I never thought about it. To me, the bigger risk would be not obeying the Lord, who was supernaturally guiding my steps and anointing everything I put my hands to.

> *God gets the glory when He intervenes to do the improbable and the impossible.*

Every decision seemed so important. God revealed that many of my early decisions would impact our business for years. Many of these early decisions can't be changed without causing other problems.

One year in, I attended a one-day seminar. That's the day I learned that 90 percent of businesses fail in the first five years. A significant percentage of those businesses had enough revenue coming in but couldn't pay their bills because of bad decisions around operating expenses. I recognized a lot of potential pitfalls but still had a lot of questions.

For example, I had to decide how much to advertise each month, which meant dealing with constant questions about ad size, days to run the ads, what kind of media (newspaper, radio, TV), and how much to spend. On the one hand it was easy to look at past results and keep doing whatever worked. But what if God had a better way? I learned to keep asking what we might do differently. And He was always faithful. Our advertising was always changing and improving.

I'll never forget our first winter. Business was great, so I substantially increased our Saturday newspaper ad size. Saturday was proving to be the best day to advertise. If we got the right placement in the paper and increased the size, the chances of people seeing the ad would increase. I woke up one Saturday excitedly, only to discover that a foot and a half of snow had fallen and was still coming down. I had difficulty getting to the store in our van, and people on the radio told everyone to stay home. My heart sank.

I had just spent most of our monthly advertising budget, and now customers couldn't even get to the store.

There I was, questioning my decision-making ability, upset that I had spent so much money on advertising, but God covered for me. That afternoon a gentleman from Canada walked into our store. He had a list of furniture he wanted to buy and a large trailer for taking it back home.

"How did you get to the store through all the snow?" I asked him in disbelief, knowing snow was usually much heavier north of Spokane.

"I didn't even see snow until I was just outside the city," he told me. "But I'd already been driving for four hours, so I wasn't going to let that stop me."

That one sale to the Canadian made the day a success. God was so faithful! He covered for the bad weather. I could almost see Him laughing as I thanked Him.

I was living out the reality of having God as my provider and problem-solver. He wanted me to invite Him into the decision-making and let

Him guide my steps. And I learned to trust Him for new ideas and better strategies to avoid problems in the first place.

God is always knocking on the door, waiting for us to hear His voice and invite Him in. He wants to walk and fellowship with us.

The only thing that can hinder this fellowship is to stop asking, expecting, and listening to His still, small voice. We need to continually open our hearts to Him and abide with Him. My part in this partnership was to press into His wisdom and trust Him, and His part was to keep giving me His "God ideas." And whether they came while I was reading His Word, listening to a sermon, driving, brushing my teeth, or taking a shower, He was faithful. I recognized His idea because His peace accompanied it.

It was important for me to remember that God was the one who always directed my steps and blessed my business. He was always there when I turned to Him. Whenever I had a major decision to make, I learned that if I took the time to wait on Him, He would direct me and guide my steps by His peace.

YOU CAN DO THE IMPOSSIBLE

God's timing and direction don't always make sense. Sometimes He shows us something we've never thought about or pictured in our imagination. Regardless of our doubt, we must trust and follow His promptings.

It's not unusual for God's guidance and direction to make little sense, considering the circumstances. He led Israel to camp by the Red Sea. Surrounded by mountains and the sea, they were seemingly trapped. Pharaoh saw their situation and pursued them, and they cried out to Moses.

It looked as if they were going to be taken captive or killed. But Moses told them, "Stand still, and see the salvation of the Lord, which He will accomplish for you today. The Lord will fight for you, and you shall hold your peace" (Exodus 14:13–14).

The solution was always there. In this case, Moses raised the rod that represented the cross of Jesus, the Red Sea parted, and the people crossed over to continue toward the promised land. God had accomplished a great miracle. What looked like certain disaster turned out to be deliverance and a history-shaping testimony.

Following God doesn't always look like the path of common sense, but He always leads us to places where He wants to do great things. I learned that trusting His direction means trusting He will be with me and fight for me just as He did on that snowy Saturday in Spokane.

God's heart has been, and will always be, to give His people answers and solutions to problems. His overall will for our lives and His specific direction gave us a huge advantage in business and life as we listened and followed. His willingness to lead us every step of the way was our greatest treasure. It was such an advantage to allow Him to guide my business and discover that was His desire. He wanted to develop me and the business in ways far beyond anything I could have done alone.

When Jesus was at a wedding with His mother, the hosts ran into a major problem when they ran out of wine—a huge embarrassment. Mary knew immediately how to solve the problem. She had watched Jesus grow up and knew what He could do. She told Him about the situation and then went to the servants and said, "Whatever He says to you, do it" (John 2:5). She knew that when you do what Jesus says, problems get resolved. He's the one with solutions.

We have an unfair advantage. We will often be successful in life simply because we follow Him.

Peter learned to do what Jesus said. When Jesus walked on water, Peter wasn't sure of what he was seeing. "Lord, if it is You, command me to come to You on the water," he said (Matthew 14:28). He knew that if Jesus told him to walk on water, it could be done. He began understanding that he could do the impossible if he partnered with God. When Jesus told him to come, Peter got out of the boat and stepped onto the waves. As long as he kept his focus on Jesus and not on the storm, he walked on water. Jesus's hand was right there to help him.

God is faithful to direct our steps whenever we ask. His answer may not always come in the way we want it or when we want it, but He will always answer.

PROBLEMS AND SOLUTIONS

For over forty years of business, God has faithfully spoken to me, given me ideas, and reminded me of ideas He has already given me. It's easy to say that my greatest treasure has been my relationship with Jesus; His solutions and guidance have made the business what it is today. He continues being so faithful in guiding me when I take the time to ask. I have never heard His audible voice, but He has guided my steps in so many ways—a thought has often popped into my head, a quickening or excitement has entered my spirit to try something new. And His peace has confirmed every major decision.

Sometimes He has guided me through my feelings or impressions or just a certainty or knowing. Sometimes it's been through a scripture I was reading that stimulated or confirmed a directive thought. Pam has heard words (not audibly) and seen pictures that have popped into her mind or imagination. It would have been easy over the years to make a wrong decision that harmed the success of our business. But time and time again, when I have taken major decisions to Jesus in prayer and asked His advice, He has helped me discern the right direction. I've usually asked Pam to pray too, and that's made it easier to move ahead on a matter when we have been in agreement. God was always there to guide our steps.

What are some ways that you recognize God is speaking to you? Are you faithful to notice and obediently steward the things He speaks to you?

I often rejoice in my spirit with expectation (hope) of God's goodness as I hunger for His direction. When God prompts us to do something, we have a choice. I committed to learn how to hear His voice and follow His leading and promptings. I lived with expectancy for an answer from heaven. The realization that Spokane needed an unfinished furniture store may have seemed sudden, but it came in the context of years of listening. Otherwise, I doubt I would have known it was the right business or would have immediately taken the steps to make it happen. But through pressing in, listening, and obeying, our company improved and prospered.

Following God doesn't always look like the path of common sense.

Though I knew this in my heart, I still had to be on guard, and sometimes I doubted my choices. There were times when He didn't seem to give a clear direction, and I had to battle self-doubt. Sometimes I would question whether thoughts were from God. But with God, you know you will eventually break through and win. Even if a decision is wrong, He will show you how to make it right. It's a learning process. When I made a mistake, I learned and moved on. Through it all our business changed, grew, improved, and transformed, and so did we.

I knew we would keep improving because of God's character. The Bible tells us we can be confident that when God begins a good work in us, He will complete it (Philippians 1:6). He is so faithful, and we kept increasing and improving every year with God co-laboring with us.

You make a lot of mistakes over forty years. My employees, wife, and children all know my weaknesses and imperfections. When I found myself missing the mark, I would ask God for forgiveness, turn my heart back to Him, and resolve to fulfill His plans and purposes for my life.

Looking back, I now realize that nothing could separate me from His love. He was looking not at my mistakes but at my heart and willingness to listen and obey. Again and again I reset my heart and affections on walking with Him. I tried to learn from my mistakes and to keep my life and business on track.

I had to be careful not to become proud and start trusting in my past success and decisions. Seeking Him in the morning for answers, connecting with Him, and discovering His wishes and desires for the business were a huge advantage and became a core value for me. I learned to remind myself that I had surrendered the business to Him, that we were in it together, and that His direction and advice were the source of our success.

I learned that three potential voices could come into your heart: God's, Satan's, and your own. Over time I grew aware of potential traps.

So with major decisions I kept waiting on God until I had His confirmations with His peace.

The enemy is quick to drop thoughts into our minds that interrupt our dependence on God. It's tempting to start thinking that our success comes from our ability or talents—which, of course, God gave us in the first place. It's easy to start focusing on results and levels of success rather than on the true source of success. When we are results-focused, worrying about maintaining success takes precedence over our relationship.

As with all of us, my heart could become very deceptive; I would think I was partnering with God but was instead making wrong decisions from ego-driven-soulish strategies and assumptions. When we hit a bump in the road, as we all will, we quickly discover what we're trusting in. And if we aren't trusting in God with all our heart, it shows.

I continually had to examine how often I met with God and whether I was receiving from Him and rejoicing in all He had given me. My own heart was the gauge: Was I excited about inviting Him into my problem and obeying His solution?

Along the way Jesus kept demonstrating God's provision. I knew and believed the business would be successful because I had peace and excitement in my heart. I knew that with God I could overcome all obstacles, including my inexperience. He would provide whatever the business needed. Just as He told Peter to launch into the deep and let down his nets for a catch (Luke 5:1–8), God had a plan for our business to succeed from the beginning. He knew in advance the decisions I should make, and when I listened to Him, He helped me make them.

A QUOTE ON MAKING DECISIONS

In early 2021, I gathered my staff and reported the remarkable sales we had experienced the year before. We celebrated! But I also explained that, although we sold the same merchandise as our competitors, we alone had seen growth in sales. How could that happen?

I believe it happened because God answered our prayers by His grace. We deserved *no* credit for this. Our smarts didn't earn it. God alone deserves all the glory for the remarkable blessing!

If you are a business or organizational leader with a heart committed to Christ who wants to impact this world for God, leaning on the Holy Spirit must become second nature. You must learn to listen for God's voice and then obey whatever He tells you. With that potent ingredient in the mix, the sauce you create can fuel some spectacular results." (David Green with Bill High, *Leadership Not by the Book: 12 Unconventional Principles to Drive Incredible Results.* David Green is the founder and CEO of Hobby Lobby.)

QUESTIONS TO PONDER

Do you believe God can direct you and tell you how to turn around negative circumstances you are in?

If you have felt like a failure in some areas, will you ask the Holy Spirit to show you the truth about how He sees you and His desire to partner with you in a new way?

How will you develop and maintain a hunger and expectation to hear God's direction and receive His good ideas?

"Now, therefore, listen to me, my children, for blessed are those who keep my ways. Hear instruction and be wise, and do not disdain it. Blessed is the man who listens to me, watching daily at my gates, waiting at the posts of my doors. For whoever finds me finds life, and obtains favor from the Lord.

—PROVERBS 8:32–35

TRUTH NINE

Jesus gave His life so His love could flow through us.

"[Jesus] gave Himself for us, that He might redeem us from every lawless deed and purify for Himself His own special people, zealous for good works."

—TITUS 2:14

When I opened the doors to Walker's Furniture, my heart expanded for people like never before. I understood my priority, and God gave me compassion for our customers. My business was not about selling furniture. It centered around meeting people's needs—serving them.

Our prices on high-quality unfinished furniture were 10 to 30 percent lower than those of normal furniture stores. We carried a lot of solid oak furniture that was very durable and easy to finish and repair, as opposed to finished furniture with veneers or a lacquer finish that was hard or impossible to repair if scratched or gouged. When customers found something they were interested in buying, I would give them extra discounts and free finishing supplies. Our mission was clear: to sell high-quality furniture at a great value with excellent customer service. I wanted our customers to buy with confidence.

That became our slogan: "Quality That Just Costs Less." When we made promises to customers, we fulfilled what we said. If we made mistakes, we offered more discounts to show we were sorry and cared about our customer's overall experience. And our sales kept increasing.

Back in Seattle, before we moved to Spokane, God put on my heart that I would need someone to come alongside me to grow the new company. I asked around in our small church if anyone worked in retail. I was told that Gary Absalonson worked for a fireplace shop in Everett, a Seattle suburb. I knew him only from a distance, but I could tell he was very outgoing and friendly, and I assumed he had integrity because he was attending our church.

Gary, who had grown up in Spokane, had only recently told his wife he loved Seattle and would never move back. He dreamed of owning a house on one of the beaches. But when I met with him to discuss the possible job I had in Spokane, the hair on his arms stood up, and he felt God's presence. That got his attention! Several months later, after the store in Spokane was up and running, he and Nancy made the move to work for us.

Looking back, I can easily see how God provided an amazing employee. But even more important, Gary became our general manager and, as the business grew, a partner. Gary has become a great friend and has been instrumental in the growth of our company. He has a gift of encouraging everyone around him and making people feel valued. I have always been a bit of an introvert; Gary's outgoing nature was a good compliment as he represented and carried our vision to our stores and employees. I could see his passion for our business immediately and easily trusted him.

Only eight months after we opened our first store, we opened a second. Gary encouraged me to open another location in Spokane Valley, and he became its manager. That store was very successful because of Gary and his hard work. He and other employees became integral to our growth as over the years we added more stores in other cities.

SERVING PEOPLE

I came across a book about twenty years ago that expressed well what God had been showing me about the value of our employees and communicating my appreciation for them. The book is by Mac Andersen and is titled *Companies Don't Succeed . . . People Do!* It includes about twenty one-page chapters on the importance of recognizing and appreciating employees—the people who determine your success. The first page boldly presents the main principle: "Treat your people like your customers." The second lists two golden rules:

Rule #1: A successful company can be built only one satisfied customer at a time.

Rule #2: Rule #1 can be done only with happy, motivated employees.

The Bible gives us a clear picture of valuing employees rather than controlling them. That's one of the first lessons I had to learn. It came from the story of the mother of James and John, two of Jesus's disciples, who asked if her sons could sit on Jesus's right and left in the Kingdom. People thought the Messiah would deliver the Jewish people from Roman domination and begin a new earthly Kingdom. Jesus's response must have sounded astonishing. What He said has the power to transform businesses, cities, and nations:

> "You know that the rulers of the Gentiles lord it over them, and those who are great exercise authority over them. Yet it shall not be so among you; but whoever desires to become great among you, let him be your servant. And whoever desires to be first among you, let him be your slave—just as the Son of Man did not come to be served, but to serve, and to give His life a ransom for many." (Matthew 20:25–28)

That principle helped me develop one of our company's core values: Our business is not about making money but serving others and their needs. It is centered around serving people.

In our third year, tensions flared between our warehouse/delivery people and our salespeople. They would point fingers at each other whenever we needed to address customer complaints. No one wanted to take responsibility. Our workers did not see each other as members of the same team. Each group felt their job was more important than the other, rather than recognizing both jobs as equally important for good customer service.

As I prayed for a solution to the tension, God gave me a great idea. I could start monthly bonuses to be distributed equally to employees, regardless of their jobs, because every job was critical to great customer service. I started setting monthly sales goals. If we sold $10,000 above the goal, every full-time employee got a $30 bonus. If we exceeded our goal by $50,000, each employee got $150 that month. I had to raise the goal as our sales climbed. And as our company grew, the dollar amount of the bonus went up too. My prayer was to hit our goals every month—a win for everyone involved. And most months we did! Because everyone shared in the bonuses equally, the plan fostered unity and teamwork. It reinforced the idea that everyone's job benefited our customers.

God showed me the importance of taking care of your employees.

We have used this bonus system for nearly four decades, with some minor adjustments, and have paid out well over $20 million in bonuses. In the last couple of decades we paid an average of eight monthly bonuses yearly. We also started giving year-end bonuses. God taught me very early to value our customers through valuing our employees. Because of that we have a fantastic group who work together as a team, as well as a base of very loyal customers who keep coming back to our stores.

At the time, my approach was an out-of-the-box idea. I had not heard of employees getting bonuses based on a company's monthly success. Giving away bonuses that would affect our bottom line and perhaps slow our growth seemed risky. But my prayer and desire were to respond in obedience to everything I felt God showed me. And this was an ongoing question I had to answer. Would I keep opening my heart to receive from God and allow Jesus to live through me and my business? How would I respond to an unusual request of God that didn't seem to make sense?

That question came up a lot in the Bible. God told Moses to provide water for thirsty people through a rock. When taxes were due, Jesus instructed His disciples to go to the sea, cast a hook, take the first fish they caught, open its mouth, and in it would be the shekel needed for the payment (Matthew 17:27). Joshua told Israel to walk around Jericho seven times without saying a word and then shout, "For the Lord has given you the city!"

God can prompt us to do something at any time that at first glance might seem unexpected and unconventional. But if we listen and follow His promptings, we will have an amazing and fulfilling journey. I'm glad I listened!

God has a purpose for everyone to reflect His goodness.

God's heart is for every business to positively impact its customers. So we developed a vision statement to promote great customer service:

> At Walker's Furniture and Mattress we place a high value on serving people. Everything we do comes from a belief that we can improve the lives of our coworkers, customers, and community. We want to offer an exceptional shopping and working environment that will provide solutions for customers and positively impact their lives. Our goal is to continually develop and improve our communication and relationship skills so our actions show we care. We want this positive culture to affect our customers and the communities we serve. Employees will appreciate working in Walker's culture and continue to grow and excel. Customers will become loyal fans and tell their friends and family about their great experience at our stores.

I have always valued our customers and employees and wanted to see them blessed, but my understanding increased when I started hearing about the Seven Mountains message in 2006. It was encouraging to learn that God wants His people to be involved in every sphere of societal influence, not just His church. He wants us to love each other and reflect His heart of love, creativity, and excellence in whatever we do, wherever we are. It became important to become a reflection of Him to my employees and foster an environment in which they could use their gifts and callings in the best possible way.

As noted earlier, the Seven Mountain message calls believers to have Kingdom influence in seven major spheres of society: government, media, education, economy, arts and entertainment, family, and religion. Through this paradigm many people are discovering their purpose in life—not just by being involved in church but also by serving God beyond the church in one of these mountains of influence and being empowered by Him to meet the needs of many with practical solutions. The field of harvest is clearly outside the church, so God pours His anointing on anyone bold enough to partner with Him to use the talents and abilities He has given him or her to serve others.

There is no formula for serving God. We can help and bless people in many ways. But God does have a plan and purpose for each of us—He created us with unique gifts and talents to make a difference in today's world. Many of us are positioned in our area of work for this time in history. He positions us to step out and say or do something that reveals His intentionality, care, and love. If we continually open our hearts and allow Him to come to us, His goodness will flow through us.

God loves people. He sits on the edge of His throne watching for loyal hearts in order to pour His love out on them. He can't wait to love the world through His faithful ones. His plan has always been to bless not just individuals but also nations. He wants those He blesses to bless others and partner with people who have a heart for cities, nations, and individuals.

Pam and I wanted to be part of His plan to pour out His love on people, but over the years our hearts have expanded to also bring His Kingdom to cities and nations. We chose to be a blessing and do good works, and that became our multiplication factor, even in business.

> *If we continually open our hearts to Him and allow Him to come to us, His goodness will flow through us.*

Jesus gave His life so we could have fellowship with Him. God is looking for a relationship with all who invite His Son into their hearts and allow Him to flow through them. He cares about everyone in cities and nations around the world. He hears the cries of the poor, the brokenhearted, and the oppressed. He wants to bring transformation and reformation to every city and nation.

This is why Jesus came; He gave His life to set people free and make us whole—spiritually, physically, and even financially. He sacrificed Himself to redeem us and transform anyone who wants to make a difference by helping people.

MINISTERING TO THE MULTITUDE

As our business grew, our love for people increased. This included our customers, employees, and communities in our cities and worldwide.

And God's blessing on our business continued to increase. He was partnering with us to love and help people—to advance His Kingdom. We found ourselves supporting orphanages in Africa, our local food bank, and even a worldwide ministry that has thousands of recorded miracles of physical and emotional healings over the years.

God is looking for people who will faithfully let His love flow through them to others. He will anoint people in all kinds of occupations, even owners of a small unfinished furniture store. Jesus, the Son of God, did not come to earth to establish a material or worldly Kingdom. He came to reveal and give away His Father's love. Jesus ministered to the poor, brokenhearted, oppressed, sick, orphans, and widows. Over the years it's been very rewarding to be able to support ministries financially—to meet thousands of desperate practical needs and see people experience wholeness and healing.

> *He gave His life to set people free and make people whole—spiritually, physically, and even financially.*

The Bible is filled with amazing stories of God seeing a need and then flowing through someone to minister to the multitudes—and the demonstration always revealed God's love. Jesus consistently demonstrated what He taught. For instance, we read that before He fed a multitude, He had compassion for the people because they had been with Him for three days and had nothing to eat. He told the disciples He didn't want to send them away hungry "lest they faint on the way" (Matthew 15:32). In other words,

"Let's feed all these people as we did a few days ago." The disciples questioned how they could feed so many. But Jesus did it! Can you imagine how the twelve disciples felt as God multiplied the fish and bread while they distributed it? They experienced God's love flowing through them to thousands of people. Once again Jesus demonstrated how much God cares for all people and that with Him, all things are possible.

I adopted 2 Corinthians 9:8 as a life verse to confess and pray in faith for our business: "God is able to make all grace abound toward you, that you, always having all sufficiency in all things, may have an abundance for every good work." This verse says that all of heaven's solutions, resources, and power is available for every situation and circumstance and to meet needs in your sphere of influence.

Grace is God's miraculous power for doing what we cannot do in our ability. We don't earn His grace; it's freely given and we freely receive it. I've prayed and believed God for His grace in hundreds of situations, and He has always been faithful. I believed my business was in His will and making a difference in people's lives, so I often came "boldly to the throne of grace" to "obtain mercy and find grace to help in time of need" (Hebrews 4:16).

Time after time God was with me in my failures and victories, always encouraging, leading, and guiding. I kept inviting Him to be involved in every aspect of our business to help us solve problems, make the right decisions to grow our business, and know what to do with the profits—profits that I considered to be His as well as our company's since we were in partnership together.

A QUOTE ON SERVANT LEADERSHIP

The journey of life is to move from a self-serving heart to a serving heart. You finally become an adult when you realize that life is about what you give rather than what you get.

To successfully combat temptations to be self-serving, we need daily to surrender our motives and actions to Christ as our guide and role model for how we should lead. (Ken Blanchard and Phil Hodges, *The Servant Leader: Transforming Your Heart, Head, Hands & Habits*)

QUESTIONS TO CONSIDER

In a small way, our business was part of God's master plan to fill the earth with His goodness and glory. How has God positioned you and your business to impact your employees, customers, community, city, and nation? If you're not sure, ask Him to show you!

I believe God's people are entering a time of demonstration similar to that of biblical times. He will demonstrate His love and goodness through His sons and daughters with signs and wonders. Are you ready to be used? Will you carry His presence and love into your sphere of influence and release His goodness? Will you let God purify you to become zealous for good works and demonstrate His love through you?

"If I then, your Lord and Teacher, have washed your feet, you also ought to wash one another's feet. . . . If you know these things, blessed are you if you do them."

—JOHN 13:14, 17

TRUTH TEN

God rewards good stewardship with multiplication.

"Well done, good and faithful servant; you were faithful over a few things, I will make you ruler over many things. Enter into the joy of your lord."

—MATTHEW 25:21

It's incredible to see how thoroughly God worked in our lives as I look back. Because He is timeless, He has always known about me. He was involved in my life before I was born. He went before me and began preparing the way for our business fifty years before it opened. He used many people, including my grandfathers, to influence the success of our company.

My mom's dad immigrated to the United States from Czechoslovakia during the Great Depression. I had heard stories about the Great Depression and how many people were out of work, just struggling to survive. My grandfather told me that he came to Spokane and found work wherever he could. He was fortunate to make one or two dollars a day. He said he lived on half of whatever he made in a month and saved the other half. I don't know how he could have done this without living in barns and eating only occasionally. His goal was to build a business so he could bring his wife and daughter (my grandmother and mother) to America.

As a young man, my grandfather worked on a cattle ranch and learned how to slaughter cows and prepare the meat to be preserved or eaten. After saving up enough money over six months to buy a cow, he slaughtered it and sold the meat to butcher shops. Then he saved up to buy two cows and then three. Within three years he owned a slaughterhouse of his own, eventually owning the largest slaughterhouse in Spokane. He said he was fortunate to sell his business for top value about five years before the large grocery stores came in and slaughterhouses started closing.

My grandfather continued living on half of what he made so he could invest the other half to build a business. For years he sacrificed his personal lifestyle, first for his family and then for his business. He lived with his wife and daughter in an apartment complex with eight units he owned and maintained. He also owned a commercial building that he rented out.

I heard this story when I was about twelve. Even then I knew he could have lived in a fancy Spokane house. Yet he was satisfied with his standard of living. It gave him peace of mind.

Another thing that stuck with me was how my grandfather lent money to people who could not get bank loans. Every week he received checks in the mail from those loans and his rentals. He had made a conscious decision to keep his standard of living well below his income level so that he could put his money to work to earn more.

When I opened the business in Spokane, I asked God for a financial strategy for the long-term health of my company. The first and most important decision was to determine the level of our personal and business expenses. Personally, we were essentially starting all over in our move to Spokane, so we needed to decide what our standard of living would be. I needed direction from God.

Larisa, our first daughter, was just eight months old, and I felt responsible to give my family the best life possible.

As I made those decisions, my grandfather's story came to mind. So did Jesus's words about sacrifice: "If anyone desires to come after Me, let him deny himself, and take up his cross, and follow Me" (Matthew 16:24). I was willing to sacrifice my standard of living to make sure our business would grow and still provide enough for us to be able to give.

I found a small two-bedroom apartment at a very low monthly rent. My goal was to keep our living expenses around $800 so our store would not have to pay us much initially. This was a substantial drop in our standard of living—less than one-fourth of our combined earnings in Seattle. We went from two cars and a beautiful three-bedroom house on a beltway to one car and a small two-bedroom apartment in a bad area of Spokane. But we were willing to make those sacrifices for our business to succeed and become profitable.

When we looked at our first monthly financial statement, Pam and I rejoiced because the business had made $3,000. If we had paid ourselves $4,000, we wouldn't have made any money, but we were able to increase our giving right away. We had kept our expenses in line with our sales. After we showed our statements to our banker eight months later, he thought our monthly income was impressive for a brand-new business. He gave us a credit line that provided us with a safety net, so two months later we were able to open a second store in the valley.

God had revealed a personal strategy, but I also had to develop a long-range business plan. I could easily see He was guiding my financial decisions, and while I considered myself a risk-taker, most decisions leaned toward the financially conservative side.

EVERY FINANCIAL DECISION MATTERS

It's hard to explain the confidence and peace of following His leading. Proverbs 10:22 says His blessing makes one rich and He adds no sorrow with it. John prayed that we would prosper and be in health, just as our soul prospers (3 John 2). God led me in financial decisions that worked for our good and His glory.

God cares about every area of our lives and knows how much success and prosperity we can handle emotionally. True prosperity comes with joy and peace and positively impacts us and others. We found that the most significant benefit of keeping all our expenses low, besides paying the bills on time, was that we could give generously immediately. I was having fun giving generous offerings to our church and missionaries and being able to bless others.

I've found many articles about our country's financial health and ability to control expenses over the years. One report from CNBC recently got my attention: Only 29 percent of people in the US are considered financially healthy—spending, saving, and planning in a way that will ensure long-term success. Key findings revealed that 54 percent said they were financially struggling, and 17 percent considered themselves financially vulnerable—and this was during economically good times. This financial situation can cause even more stress and potential problems in an economic downturn with the loss of jobs.

> *True prosperity comes with joy and peace and positively impacts you and others.*

Most businesses follow suit by borrowing a lot to maximize their potential for gain. Businesses are encouraged to borrow, continually taking on a lot of risk in order to grow. At first we used a credit line only in emergencies and paid it off as soon as possible. Then as we grew our business, we got a few loans that we knew we could easily make the payment on. Occasionally I would obtain large loans on my personal real estate investments (our store locations) when I was confident our company could make those rent payments as well. Walker's Furniture had always had a credit line for unusual circumstances that might come up. But over time we've been able to pay off our loans, be generous givers, and still enjoy His financial blessings.

So with God's guidance, our company developed a conservative stance on borrowing and debt. Looking back, we can see that if we had a lot of debt, we might not have survived some of the economic downturns and recessions. We were always looking for opportunities to grow, but only if we knew we could keep our expenses in line and handle the increase in business without compromising our customer service. I had been told early on that I might not make money in the first five years. But because our company kept the expenses low from the beginning, we made money our first year and every year after, even in recessions.

One valuable resource I discovered during that time was a John C. Maxwell book titled *Today Matters: 12 Daily Practices to Guarantee Tomorrow's Success.* Maxwell is a bestselling author who has written many books full of business success strategies. *Today Matters* has twelve chapters describing how good decisions today will give you a better tomorrow. Every chapter is excellent. When I opened my store I had never heard of John Maxwell, so I must give God the credit for establishing many of the concepts in this book in my heart before I even read it.

John Maxwell stresses that the secret of our success is determined by our daily agenda. Three chapters on finances, generosity, and growth highlight the importance of daily financial decisions. God revealed to us how important it was to manage our finances and profits properly—that every financial decision mattered—so we could be generous and at the same time grow the company by keeping our personal expenses very low. Many of the financial decisions (sacrifices) my wife and I made in those first years greatly impacted the long-term success of our company. Still, forty years later, we keep our personal expenses very low compared to our income so we can be generous givers.

PEACE OF MIND

Partnering with God in business is amazing. Together we've developed a long-term strategy on how to steward our profits—His and mine—at year-end: paying our bills on time, then paying our personal and business taxes, and then giving bonuses and raises to our employees. We had three equally important financial goals: to invest back into our business so that it continued growing, to support ministries to advance God's Kingdom, and to enjoy God's blessings as a family. Every year was different, depending on how God directed and what opportunities were available. But because of His favor and blessing, the percentages of money distributed to four areas have been relatively consistent:

- Business and personal taxes: 30–35 percent
- Investing back into the business or real estate: 20–30 percent
- Giving to ministries: 20–30 percent

- Paying our personal bills: 20–30 percent

I'm not claiming that this is a formula for guaranteed success, only that this is how God guided us in our retail business. It's a formula that has given me peace and joy.

I've tried not to evaluate success from our sales or how much I've given or accumulated. I'm simply aware that true success comes from walking with God. I remind myself often that my success can be evaluated only through my ongoing relationship with Jesus and how I've stewarded the gifts and talents God has given me. I hope to hear Him tell me one day that I've been a faithful steward of all He has given me. He has been so faithful in fulfilling His promise to give me the ability to get wealth. I know I've been given much, and much will be required. I want to be faithful in helping establish His covenant.

God went before me and prepared the way, using my grandfather to give me a great business strategy. God revealed how we could be generous givers and grow our business simultaneously. And He has been faithful to multiply our resources over the years.

He rewards faithful stewards.

Being financially conservative from the beginning impacted the business's success, but most importantly, our peace of mind. That financial strategy gave me a significant advantage in business and life. Keeping our expenses in line by always having very little debt and by controlling our overall costs with God's help and direction helped me deal with setbacks and problems emotionally. Every year I've experienced the joy of being able to give bonuses and raises.

> **I've tried not to evaluate success from our sales or how much I've given or accumulated. I'm simply aware that true success comes from walking with God.**

God promises that He will keep in perfect peace the mind that is stayed on Him and trusts in Him (Isaiah 26:3). I had that peace. The conservative financial policy God gave us made all the difference in knowing what to say yes or no to in our decision-making.

That doesn't mean I never made any bad financial decisions. I've regretted some personal investments I made outside of our business. Most of them came after years of success and being a little overconfident. Some investments in a gold mine, an oil well, stocks, trading options, and currencies haven't worked out well. But I realized I made them out of pride. Because of our success in business, I assumed God would bless me in other ways, and those investments were made without getting His confirmation.

In a passage that ends with a warning that God resists the proud and a promise that He gives grace to the humble, James warned us about trying to be successful without the right motivations (James 4:1–8). I've learned over the years that success can influence our decisions and ability to hear God.

Past financial successes don't automatically spill over into all other investments. Just because an opportunity sounds good does not mean it's God's will. He wants us to prosper on the inside above all, and only then is outward prosperity good for us. As the Proverb noted earlier says, "The blessing of the Lord makes one rich, and He adds no sorrow with it" (Proverbs 10:22).

Don't let the deceitfulness of riches and the cares of the world influence or change your business strategy or your desire to advance the Kingdom of God. Since I aligned with the desire to hear from the Lord that I was a faithful steward, we tried making choices for the long haul. We wanted to finish strong. We established in our hearts the principle of pursuing the long-term health of our company and employees so we could continue growing and having an impact.

Money does not bring true joy and fulfillment—if it isn't stewarded well, it becomes a trap of greed and self-gratification. The joy comes from partnering with God to fulfill our purpose and destiny and make a difference. We are God's workmanship, created for good works in Christ, that God has prepared beforehand (Ephesians 2:10). Being in business for forty years and trying to steward it well under His direction has been an incredible journey.

He wants us to prosper on the inside above all, and only then is outward prosperity good for us.

A QUOTE ON STEWARDSHIP

God wants partners. I didn't originate this idea with my parable—Jesus did it with His.

He used the parable of stewardship to describe how His Kingdom comes: By giving His servants money to handle, the Master is looking to find those who can rule faithfully with Him in His Kingdom (see Luke 19:11–27). The reward of faithfulness is to share in the King's authority—in fact, to be part of His family business. Our stewardship is "training for reigning."

As we see in most areas of life, we train for something simply by doing it. We can learn a lot about something without doing it, but we only learn to do it by doing it. (Stephen K. De Silva, *Money and the Prosperous Soul: Tipping the Scales of Favor and Blessing*)

QUESTIONS TO CONSIDER

Do you have any financial decisions that you regret? Do you see a connection between those and some potentially wrong motivations—pride or presumption? Confess those to Him today and recommit to the ways He desires to bless you that indeed "[add] no sorrow with it."

He has done exceedingly abundantly above all we've ever asked or even thought by His power working within us (Ephesians 3:20). Are you ready to experience that reality in your business partnership with God? Ask Him for the next step and faithfully obey His direction daily, and see what happens when your faithful stewardship meets His power that is working within you!

"Now he who received seed among the thorns is he who hears the word, and the cares of this world and the deceitfulness of riches choke the word, and he becomes unfruitful. But he who received seed on the good ground is he who hears the word and understands it, who indeed bears fruit and produces: some a hundredfold, some sixty, some thirty."

—MATTHEW 13:22–23

TRUTH ELEVEN

When you're partnered with God, adversity makes you stronger.

"We also glory in tribulations, knowing that tribulation produces perseverance; and perseverance, character; and character, hope. Now hope does not disappoint, because the love of God has been poured out in our hearts by the Holy Spirit who was given to us."

—ROMANS 5:3–5

If you compared our first furniture store, which opened in 1980, with other furniture stores in Spokane, we would have looked like a two-year-old competing against giants. The largest store in the city was about 100,000 square feet, with an additional store almost half that size north of the city. It was a chain and the most dominant furniture retailer in the area. There were three other large stores—around 40,000 square feet each. Then there were the smaller independent furniture stores. Add to that the well-established department stores that had furniture departments. In all, I would guess there were about twenty prominent stores displaying furniture in nearly half a million square feet. Our store was 2,000 square feet of unfinished furniture with no sofas, loveseats, or anything upholstered.

Talk about small beginnings!

None of the twenty stores were concerned about us because we didn't look very threatening. They filled weekend newspapers with full-page ads offering a wide selection of furniture at great prices. We had a small advertising budget—between two and three thousand dollars.

As I observed what these stores were doing and learned from them, I never feared their size or advertising ability. God and I were a team. It was His idea to open our store, so I kept believing and receiving His help to grow our company. Even though we were the smallest furniture store, I never took on the identity of being weak or somehow inferior. My identity was working with Him, which gave me complete confidence in our ability to grow.

I felt like Joshua and Caleb when they were trying to convince Israel to take the promised land (Numbers 14:8–9). Yes, there were giants, but with God's favor and blessing, we would continue growing and gaining market share.

In the first ten years of business we kept improving our product mix and began accessorizing our stores. Pam was very involved and bought accessories to help our displays. Most popular upholstery lines were not available for our company to buy and sell, so God led me to Stylecraft, a new line recently available on the West Coast. It eventually grew to be one of the most dominant upholstery lines in the country. Our resources kept expanding. I had no fear, just excitement and confidence in where we were headed with God's help.

> *My identity was working with Him, which gave me complete confidence in our ability to grow.*

We constantly looked for ways to improve our stores. We expanded their size, opened in other markets, and kept changing and improving our advertising, pointing out our advantages over other stores in the area. We set up displays at interstate fairs and were constantly educating people about the advantages of buying solid oak. After ten years we had started selling finished furniture as well and were doing $10 million a year with four stores. We were very excited about what God was doing with our company!

COMPETITION

In 1991, after eleven years in business, a major competitor opened in our market. It sold furniture, mattresses, and appliances in a big way. They had tons of money for advertising and ran about ten times more ads than we did. They were all over TV, showing off their large, beautiful store. The company created quite a stir in our market. They advertised some exceptional loss leaders—furniture that is significantly lower in cost than what other stores advertise—therefore, our advertising suddenly had minimal impact.

I had to make a choice. Should I concede some of the market share we had worked so hard to establish, or should I press into God to see how we could stay competitive and keep growing? We were led to improve our product mix to remain competitive and continued reminding everyone that we had the best quality at the best prices. Instead of pulling back, we learned how to improve our advertising and stay competitive. We gave bigger discounts and continued offering incredible value to every customer.

In 1994 we heard that this giant competitor was opening another Spokane Valley store close to one of our locations. So we just pressed in harder for God's favor and direction. Then suddenly in 1996 they closed their doors and declared bankruptcy. With the competitor removed, unhappy customers came to our stores for help. God had used the adversity during this time to strengthen our stores. It forced us to improve every aspect of our operations and prepared us for the next level in sales and customer service.

When stores started opening in our markets advertising Tempur-Pedic mattresses, a new technology that offered better sleep, it caught everyone's attention. We wanted to take advantage of the popularity of this technology breakthrough, so we opened several mattress stores in our region—but not under the Walker's name. We sold a lot of mattresses at those stores, but the sales created much more work and were not very profitable. Mattress sales at Walker's stores also began suffering, so we decided to sell those mattress stores.

God prompted me to expand our mattress displays inside our Walker's locations. We made beautiful displays for them and nearly tripled the number of mattresses we carried. We sold a variety. We made beautiful displays and moved them to more prominent areas in our stores so customers would see them. We trained our salespeople and increased our mattress advertising. Our mattress sales doubled over time, and we were able to advertise regionally. We had once been happy with a thousand-dollar mattress sale, but with adjustable bases and better quality, a mattress might sell for three to five times that amount. And our customers were happy to pay that much for a better night's sleep. Mattress sales benefited their health and our success.

Mattress Firm, the largest mattress company in the country, had been dominating sales on the East Coast. Then they started buying large mattress chains on the West Coast. Before we knew it, fifteen of their stores were in our region, and their advertising equaled that of our furniture and mattresses advertising budget. They were a giant in the industry—carrying the best brands, experiencing annual sales of around two billion dollars, and developing top-of-mind awareness among customers. They confidently told customers who walked into their stores that they were the best. And when it comes to sales, they were. They sold more mattresses than anyone else in the country. They seemed to have unlimited finances and clout and kept opening new stores in our market area.

We again had some decisions to make. Should we pull back on our mattress promotions and emphasize our furniture instead? Should we just concede our mattress market share to this billion-dollar company? We decided to keep growing our mattress sales. We remodeled some of our stores, redid our mattress displays, improved our mattress galleries, and dramatically bumped up our mattress ads.

We began spending half our advertising budget on mattress advertising. The manufacturer we had been buying from for years started giving us more advertising co-op money. It also had a new line of mattresses that were competitive with Tempur-Pedic. We simply kept pressing into what God was prompting us to do. The competition drove us to increase mattress sales, which have become very important to the success of our business. On the other hand, Mattress Firm eventually filed for bankruptcy and closed some of its stores in our market.

Adversity can hurt or help you. It all depends on whether you take on the challenge to improve and the risk to compete. Looking back on it now, I can see how adversity brought our company to a new level. We believed God would anoint what we put our hands to and that we would continue being successful. He did, and we have.

More recently, Internet sales have become our next significant threat, and our industry is concerned about the impact. But with God on our side, we will continue growing. And I've finally begun seeing these challenges as a benefit because God always strengthens Walker's to keep going to new levels. Nothing can stop us from fulfilling His plans for our lives as we continue walking with Him.

GOD ON YOUR SIDE

Adversity makes us stronger when we humbly draw near to God. Our competition forced us to get better in every facet of our business. I continually believed that all things work for the good of those who love God, and I confessed and believed that somehow, some way, God would turn the situation around.

When other businesses that appear to be very successful move into your area, you have three options. You can slow down, take a conservative approach, and try to exist as long as possible. You can work long hours, cut back, and do everything you can to keep growing and competing. Or—and this is the best option—you can keep believing God is your partner and invite Him into the middle of your circumstances. You can stand on His promises, knowing that He is your strength and provider and that He fights for you.

Adversity can hurt you or help you. It all depends on whether you take on the challenge.

Together we get through. With Him at our side our perspective changes, and our options to keep growing and improving are unlimited. When we get promptings and ideas that give us peace, we can follow His leading.

God's Word is alive and powerful, and we can partner with His divine nature through His great promises, calling those things that do not exist into existence (Hebrews 4:12; 2 Peter 1:4; Romans 4:17).

I have established so many wonderful promises deep in my heart, believing and holding onto them until I saw breakthrough. Paul wrote of looking not at things that are seen but at things that are not seen. He was saying that we should not define our reality by focusing on our circumstances—but by faith seeing God's promises in His eternal Word as our reality. Again and again I have established a promise in my heart, not just my head, and seen God come through. Our business has overcome many adverse situations as we have confessed and believed His promises.

I continually meditated on God's promises, confessing and believing them until I knew deep in my heart that God would turn the situation around. And He has. I've seen Him turn many dire, seemingly impossible circumstances in our business into something good. God can do what He has promised and invites us to hold onto our confession. When we ask according to His will, He hears us.

By faith we can cease trying to overcome obstacles in our strength and stand on His Word and promises, overcoming from a place of faith rather than fear. Knowing that God will fulfill His Word and promises keeps us on track. He is so faithful to establish His goodness in our lives. When we know that our motivation for our occupation is to help people and advance His Kingdom, it's easy to believe His promises and experience fulfillment.

Most of the time circumstances did not change how I hoped, but many actually turned out better. Stiff competition took our business to a higher level. Partnering with God in business has been an amazing relationship because He continually breathes His resurrection life into our business to turn circumstances around. And we continue meeting our goal—He is working in us to advance His Kingdom.

A QUOTE ON OVERCOMING OBSTACLES

There is no economic crisis on earth that God has not already placed the solution for in His sons and daughters who are willing to co-labor with Him. There is no economic crisis that will ever come that He won't already have the solution for, available through His kids. We simply need to awaken to who He is and what He is all about and then arise and shine with what He has given us. (Johnny and Elizabeth Enlow, *RISE: A Reformer's Handbook for the Seven Mountains*)

QUESTIONS TO CONSIDER

Have you felt overwhelmed by the success of others around you, as if you are too small to make a difference? Pray for your competition, forgiving them for any way they have tried to hurt your business. Invite the Holy Spirit today to teach you not to dread challenges but to embrace them as an opportunity to grow and become stronger.

What obstacles do you currently see in your business? Can you think of a couple of key scriptures you could write down and focus on daily to help you stay in a place of faith until you see Him turn your situation around?

"We know that all things work together for good to those who love God, to those who are the called according to His purpose."

—ROMANS 8:28

TRUTH TWELVE

Forgiveness opens the door for God's favor to flow.

"Blessed is he who is not offended because of Me."
—MATTHEW 11:6

For fourteen years after our grand opening, our sales grew an average of 30 percent yearly. We had six stores doing everything needed to keep up with growth and keep our customers happy. My partner and general manager, Gary, did a great job opening stores and training our managers and employees to keep everything running smoothly. He handled all major customer problems as we developed company policies. I oversaw all the operations at our distribution center, including advertising, merchandise buying, and all major financial decisions. We made a great team, so I decided to give Gary a bonus of company shares.

You can imagine my surprise when he walked into my office and said he wanted to move to Montana so he could open his own store. I was stunned. I just assumed he would be with our company for forty years.

Many years prior, Gary had moved to our first store outside of Spokane when it first started. He was so committed and instrumental in making our company a success, and now I wondered how we would handle it all without him. One of the reasons I opened all these stores was that I knew Gary was anointed to oversee them.

This was one of the moments I prayed earnestly to God.

"I'm glad we are partners in this business together because I need Your help."

It would have been easy to be upset with Gary and try making him feel obligated to our company and employees. I could have held a grudge and tried to make it hard for him to open a new store. But being partnered with God forced me to look at the situation through His eyes. God had encouraged Gary to be part of our business, so I had to believe He had a plan for Gary in his business—and a plan to replace Gary.

Fortunately, God had prepared me for this moment. Years earlier I had done the very same thing Gary decided to do.

"I want to move to Spokane in nine months to open my own store," I told my Seattle boss.

I explained how committed I was to his store and how hard I would continue working for him during the months I would still be there.

"When you find a new manager for the store, I'll train him," I said.

I assured him that I did not want him to lose sales because of my new move and would ensure sales continued increasing and the store ran smoothly.

My boss promptly fired me the following day.

It totally surprised me. I always questioned why it happened; it was not part of my plan. Pam had just had our first child and had retired from her teaching job. Suddenly we were both out of work. Was I still supposed to open in Spokane the following summer? I reminded God that we were opening the business together. I had to move forward and get a job to pay our bills. Our house also needed to be sold before we moved. We had a lot of commitments, and I needed God's direction.

Within one week I had a construction job that paid great, and Pam eventually got a waitressing job at a bowling alley at night. Whoever wasn't working could take care of our new daughter, Larisa.

In that season God gave me the grace to see the whole thing from my boss's viewpoint. He was thinking about the future of his business. He had trained me, invested a lot of time and money in me, and given me a lot of responsibility. Why should he keep investing in me if I was going to leave? How could he know I would continue working as hard as I said I would? For all he knew, I would spend time planning my new store while working. I could understand why he might not want me to train the next manager.

How could I be upset? I had told him nine months early because I cared about him, his company, and their success. Most importantly, I did not want to walk away from the job and our friendship with any hurt feelings between us. I knew how important it was to forgive and not hold grudges. Many testimonies I had heard spoke about how critical it is to guard our hearts by forgiving and not holding grudges.

I will never forget a testimony about a business being threatened in every possible way by its competitor, and the owner began thinking about closing his store. He asked for prayer from a group of businessmen, and in prayer they heard from God that the key to his breakthrough was to forgive the other owner. So the business owner prayed for his competitor and forgave him for all the ways the man had hurt his business. He felt a heavy weight fall off his shoulders. About a month later the competitor called and said he was closing his store and wanted to sell the man all his inventory at a reduced price.

It was a miracle—a turnaround from being a fierce competitor to being a complete blessing.

Forgiveness always opens the door for God to move. Remember: Jesus said to love our enemies and pray for them, that if anyone sues you for your tunic, you should also let the person have your cloak, or when we're asked to go one mile, to go two (Matthew 5:39–42). Jesus taught us how to break free from grudges and bitterness that can otherwise keep us in bondage.

It was a big blow when Gary told me he was going to Montana. I had always known God brought Gary to me. Yet as I thought about the time I had been fired because of my hopes and dreams of building a store, I realized it was not for me to question Gary's decision or try to discourage him. I saw his ability and potential, so who was I to hold him back from starting his own business in a state where I would not be opening a store?

Instead of harboring any ill will toward Gary, I decided to help him however I could and work with his timeline. I knew he could be a success. But I could not buy his shares back because the company did not have the extra cash due to our expansion. I was determined not to have any hard feelings, and I told Gary I would try to buy his shares as soon as possible. He agreed and eventually moved to Missoula to open a store.

Forgiveness always opens the door for God to move.

Now my hands were full with six stores and no general manager to handle the significant problems. I was just holding on, waiting to see what God would do. I asked how to replace Gary and looked for ways to streamline our stores.

About a year after Gary opened his store, he came back to Spokane and asked if he could meet with me. I thought he might ask me to buy back some of his stock. To my surprise, he wanted his job back and said he would like to continue earning shares in our company. I was ecstatic! I agreed, of course, and we were back together as a team.

The great part of this story is that Gary came back more committed and energized to do a great job. He was an even better general manager than before. He now understood and appreciated both of our roles and was ready to take our company to a new level. Not holding a grudge against him left an open door for him to return. God is so good! His ways are amazing.

God has brought me some fantastic employees who have taken our company to levels of success I could not have accomplished on my own. As our company has grown, every job has become more specialized, and many of our employees have found their perfect fit. Darcy has become an amazing controller, Cynthia an excellent buyer, and our managers are excelling in their jobs.

Sales reps who visit our stores always comment on how great our managers are and are impressed by how long so many have been with us. To this day many of Walker's key employees have worked for us between twenty-five and forty years.

GUARD YOUR HEART

Jesus came to earth and gave His life to free us from anger, bitterness, unforgiveness, and selfishness. He once forgave a crippled man for his sins before healing his body (Mark 2:1–12). God cares about the condition of your heart and your relationship with Him over your success.

Scripture says to guard our hearts (Proverbs 4:23). John prayed that his friend would prosper in health and in all things "just as your soul prospers" (3 John 2). What is inside our hearts eventually shapes our lives and work. A diseased tree cannot bear good fruit, but a healthy tree will bear good fruit. Reaping what we sow is a simple truth (Galatians 6:7). If we sow fear, anger, unforgiveness, and control, then that is what we will reap. If we sow love, encouragement, forgiveness, and blessing in those around us, then that's what we will reap.

Describing this Kingdom cycle, Jesus said that if we don't judge and condemn, we won't be judged and condemned. We will be forgiven if we forgive. "Give, and it will be given to you: good measure, pressed down, shaken together, and running over will be put into your bosom. For with the same measure that you use, it will be measured back to you" (Luke 6:38). Whatever you give comes back to you in abundance.

As we saw earlier, this passage is talking not just about money. Its focus is on how we handle our relationships and what comes out of our hearts. God always looks at the heart, just as He did with David, a man after God's heart. David wasn't perfect—he did some terrible things—but he was quick to repent. He was known for praising God and writing about his desire to be with God and do God's will.

You will make mistakes. We all do. But God will walk with you through any trial if your priority is to walk with Him, follow His ways, and let Him direct your steps. If you let circumstances cause discouragement, bitterness, or unforgiveness, that's what will come out in your life and work. But if you forgive and offer others the same grace you've been given, God can take your life and work to a whole new level.

As your business grows, so does the level of stress. I needed to guard my heart and watch what was coming out of my mouth. The Lord's Prayer tells us to ask forgiveness for our debts as we forgive our debtors, so I prioritized asking forgiveness for all my sins and faults. But I needed more than forgiveness; I had to change. I made many mistakes in life and business and continually had to ask God to forgive and cleanse me of these faults. I knew I had to change my ways, or people in my personal and work life would be affected.

Offsenses will hinder our relationship with God.

It was also vital for me to be quick to forgive and to constantly examine my heart, to know that no "root of bitterness" would spring up and cause trouble (Hebrews 12:15). We cannot afford to hold grudges. We must watch what enters our hearts because whatever we let in eventually emerges.

Something occurs every day in business that can harden a heart. There's pressure to keep improving, avoid mistakes, and be successful. Opportunities for hurt feelings among vendors, customers, and employees are everywhere. It's easy to get upset and blame someone else for problems. I often called vendors to tell them I needed a solution to a problem, but I couldn't allow myself to become bitter when problems arose.

It's too easy to get angry and say something you don't want to. I quickly realized how important it was to forgive others and guard my thoughts and words. I didn't want to do or say something I would regret. And when I did, I wanted to admit I was wrong and quickly apologize. It's an important value to develop—one I'm still working on today.

A QUOTE ON FORGIVENESS

Unconditional forgiveness becomes an essential part of our lifestyle, and this paves the way for an even greater outpouring of God's mercy and grace upon us. But we must be aware that any unforgiveness in our life will have the opposite effect—it will short-circuit the power of the Kingdom in our lives and will prevent the blessing of God from flowing. Unforgiveness is perhaps the number one grace blocker in a person's spiritual life. (John and Carol Arnott, *Grace & Forgiveness: A Powerful Key to Your Freedom and Healing*. John and Carol are founding pastors of Catch the Fire and overseers of the Partners in Harvest network of churches and international speakers.)

QUESTIONS TO CONSIDER

Are there places of offense in your heart and in relationships within your family or business that could be blocking the blessing of God? Would you choose today to forgive and bless them, trusting that the access that our enemy, the devil, has had will be stopped so God can deal with them in His way and time?

Is there a situation in your life or business that could be resolved or improved with an apology from you? Is there some action you can take or words you could express that would bring more unity and peace into your workplace? Lean on God as your partner and ask Him for humility and wisdom.

"Keep your heart with all diligence, for out of it spring the issues of life. Put away from you a deceitful mouth, and put perverse lips far from you."

—PROVERBS 4:23–24

TRUTH THIRTEEN

God has given us access to His love and grace.

"Let us therefore come boldly to the throne of grace, that we may obtain mercy and find grace to help in time of need."

—HEBREWS 4:16

When working full-time I loved to read the Bible at home whenever possible, usually early in the morning. While traveling I took Christian books with me, looking for testimonies and insights from Scripture that would transform me. I wasn't just reading to gain knowledge; my goal was always that my heart and life might be changed.

The Word of God is alive and powerful and has had such an impact on me. It is full of powerful promises. I have always believed the Holy Spirit highlights Scripture to help me through life. There are many truths I have meditated on and confessed, truths that have washed over my heart and soul. Over time as I have done this, my life has changed. His Word would enter my mind and heart, eventually turning my thoughts into words. Then my words would become actions; actions turned into habits, and habits developed into a lifestyle.

One memorable morning I was rereading a book that discussed a way to hear from what you see. You can see what God is saying to you through visions, dreams, and your God-inspired imagination—it was new to me.

Imagination is not inherently bad; we have a choice to use it for good or for evil. Ask God to sanctify your imagination for His use. You can picture anything in your imagination—a pink elephant holding an umbrella and walking on a tightrope a hundred feet above the ground, for example. So why not let our imagination be used by God instead of the enemy? And that was the idea I found encouraging within the book. It quoted the prophet Habakkuk: "I will stand my watch and set myself on the rampart, and watch to see what He will say to me, and what I will answer when I am corrected" (Habakkuk 2:1). Our imagination can impact our heart and who we become. As one translation of a proverb says, "For as [a man] thinks in his heart, so is he" (Proverbs 23:7).

The book was full of wonderful testimonies of lives being changed when people waited to see what God would say. That was totally out of the box for me. I was more of an analytical thinker. But the book was inspiring, so I told God, "I will try this. I'll wait to see what You will say to me."

After sitting in a chair, I tried to remove any thoughts as I waited on God. My mind became a blank canvas as five minutes passed, then ten. Suddenly I could picture standing on a beach. Nearby waves crashed onto rocks. As I looked down at the sand and the sea, I saw someone approaching. As the person walked toward me, I wondered if this could be Jesus.

It was. He walked right up to me, and I heard His words in my mind. "Do you know how much I love you?"

I replied with the first thing that came to my mind. "I know you gave your life to save the world so that those who believe in you will not perish."

He looked at me and asked it again. "Do you know how much I love you?"

I paused momentarily, then said, "I know you love me so much that you gave your life just for me. You went through that horrific death on the cross and would have done it just for me."

Then Jesus looked at me again and said a third time, "Do you know how much I love you?"

If He had to ask me three times, I apparently didn't have a clue. Another thought crossed my mind as I wondered what to say and how to answer.

Am I making this all up? Is this really happening?

Then Jesus knelt, touched both my feet, looked up at me, and said, "You will know that this really happened because your feet are healed." Then the vision was gone.

For about twenty years I had struggled with athlete's foot, especially between my smallest two toes. No matter how many different powders and creams I tried, it always came back. But to my surprise it was gone after this vision and has not returned.

Jesus reminded me of His love and demonstrated it, just as He demonstrated His love on the cross for all. He wants the world to believe and receive all His love and all that He did on the cross. He became the mediator of a better covenant established on better promises (Hebrews 8:6).

REMINDERS OF GOD'S LOVE

God is always talking; I just had to take the time to see what He was saying. Paul wrote about this in his amazing prayer for the Ephesians. He prayed that God would strengthen them with might through His Spirit in their inner being, that God's fullness would dwell in their hearts through faith (Ephesians 3:16–19). To know the love of Christ, it helps to understand what He is saying. We must learn how He speaks to us.

It's like a sailboat in the wind. It will not move if its sails are not out to catch the wind. In the same way, we must anticipate hearing God when we tune in to His language. We also need to know the characteristics in His voice, whether in a vision, our thoughts, or an impression in our hearts. His voice is edifying, truthful, positive, and full of love, and it brings peace. His voice will never accuse or demean, and it will never make us feel condemned. We may feel convicted that something in our lives needs to change. God is there for us at every step.

When we behold Jesus and encounter His love, His promises come alive. I was convinced that God would be faithful to fulfill what He had promised. If we knew how much Jesus loved us, we would receive all He did on the cross by faith, hold fast to the confession of hope (His promises), and bind them to our hearts until we are fully convinced that He will fulfill His promises in our lives. The Bible says we partake or partner with God's divine nature and escape the corruption of the world through His precious promises (2 Peter 1:4). There are so many of them in our Bible, and I was being challenged. Was I partnering with all God's promises and all Jesus did for me on the cross? I had to examine my heart. I needed help to put off the old man and put on the new man—to put on Christ.

To know the love of Christ, it helps to understand what He is saying.

We must know how He speaks to us.

God's heart is always to redeem and restore. In our time of need we can, by faith, come boldly to the throne of mercy and grace.

Jesus sacrificed His life so we could put on His life, clothe ourselves in His life, and live, move, and have our being in Him. He demonstrated His love to me just as He demonstrated His love to the world. Through His death and resurrection I could live in Him by faith, and so can you. Paul counted everything a loss so he might gain Christ and be found in Him (Philippians 3:8–10). What an amazing offer!

In three years of ministry Jesus manifested God's heart to bless and set us free from bondage. He is now the mediator of a better covenant established on better promises. We can have direct access to God and connect to His love and His promises any time of the day.

No matter what was going on in my life or how busy I was, I needed to spend time in God's Word and sit at His feet, receiving from Him. I had to take time to fall into His arms and rest in His love—to open my heart to listen to Him, to listen to what He was saying and how He was directing my steps.

It is vital "to know the love of Christ which passes knowledge" (Ephesians 3:19), and it's impossible to know His love in our minds until we open our hearts to experience and receive His help to make changes in our lives. God has encouraged me in the last few years through license plate numbers or the time on a clock. I look up the numbers for potential promises in Psalms or Isaiah. Certain numbers are a reminder of His love; my wife says they are like a kiss from heaven. Paying attention to what God is saying—looking to see how He is speaking—is one of the ways we become more aware of His love.

God's heart is always to redeem and restore.

GRATITUDE

In Jewish culture you prove you know and understand something only when your actions are altered. It is not considered knowledge until you put it into practice. In *RISE: A Reformer's Handbook for the Seven Mountains,* authors Johnny and Elizabeth Enlow write about a key statement that helps us intentionally step into this:

"I live . . .

to know the real Him,

to make the real Him known, and to learn to love and be loved."

This is not just about head knowledge. God is looking for people who form a personal relationship with Him, know and experience His love, and then allow His love to flow through them to others. Rejoicing and acknowledging all He has done for me ignites His love to flow through me. Psalm 103 is an excellent example of remembering who God is so that His love flows in and through us. It reveals a God who "forgives all your iniquities, who heals all your diseases, who redeems your life from destruction, who crowns you with lovingkindness and tender mercies, who satisfies your mouth with good things, so that your youth is renewed like the eagle's" (Psalm 103:3–5).

I often go on and on thanking Him and rejoicing in all He has done in my life. As I encounter and experience His love, I am challenged to let His love pour into me and through me, to be loved and to love.

You can also experience His love for you in a real way today. Begin by expressing your gratitude to Him. Then allow your heart, not just your mind, to be aware of God's heart toward you. Get still on the inside, dedicate the screen of your imagination to Him, and ask Him to show you a picture of what He wants to say to you today. Don't forget to write it down as an ongoing encouragement, no matter how simple it may be.

As with anything else He gives us, God will trust us with more as we are faithful with the little things.

A QUOTE ON GOD'S LOVE

One of the more meaningful parts of my life is the five-minute vacations I take. They can happen anytime or anywhere. The amount of time I take varies, but the activity does not. For example, if I'm in my office, I'll ask my secretary to hold my calls for a few minutes. I will sit down and generally close my eyes and pray something like this: "God, I'm going to sit here quietly, just to be the object of your love." The flow of His love for us is huge, likened to the water that flows over Niagara Falls—except Niagara is too small. Becoming aware of that love and experiencing that love is wonderful beyond words. It has the side benefit of driving out all fear.

There are only two basic emotions in life: love and fear. Turning my attention toward His love for me only increases my love for Him. It's an unending love fest where I delight in Him. . . . He is the ultimate pleasure and must be treasured as such." (Bill Johnson, *Hosting His Presence: Unveiling Heaven's Agenda.* Bill was a fifth-generation pastor with a rich heritage in the Holy Spirit. Together Bill and his wife served a growing number of churches that have partnered for revival.)

QUESTIONS TO CONSIDER

What specific areas in your business require God's help right now? What could it look like if you obtained mercy and grace from God related to those things? Communicate your needs to God boldly, asking Him for the help you need.

> *"If by the one man's offense death reigned through the one, much more those who receive abundance of grace and of the gift of righteousness will reign in life through the One, Jesus Christ."*
>
> —ROMANS 5:17

TRUTH FOURTEEN

God is looking for people who will allow His generosity to flow through them.

"He who sows sparingly will also reap sparingly, and he who sows bountifully will also reap bountifully. So let each one give as he purposes in his heart, not grudgingly or of necessity; for God loves a cheerful giver."

—2 CORINTHIANS 9:6–7

After being in business for twenty-five years, we could clearly see God's hand on our business. Our sales increased between 10 and 30 percent almost every year, and we were able to handle the growth. The few years our sales did not grow, our profits still grew because we were able to become more efficient and keep our expenses in line. Year after year because of God's blessing, we were able to give our employees yearly raises and, in most months, generous bonuses.

I was also excited because God blessed our real estate purchases that we owned separately from our company. They were bringing in a steady income. Our rental income coupled with our company's success gave us the ability to give substantially to God's Kingdom. In our opening month we cheerfully gave around 20 to 30 percent of our personal income, although that wasn't very much at first. Our giving was a priority, and it served as our primary motivation to grow our business when opportunities came our way. We continued giving similar percentages of our personal income joyfully and cheerfully as God led us each year.

Giving so blessed Pam and me that it became a lifestyle, and it rarely felt like a necessity or obligation. We experienced the promise of 2 Corinthians 9:8: "God is able to make all grace abound toward you, that you, always having all sufficiency in all things, may have an abundance for every good work." I began meditating on this and confessing it all the time. I prayed this verse and asked for God's grace to help us fulfill our destiny. I reminded God that we were in this business together, and I desperately needed Him to partner with me to do the impossible.

Giving so blessed [us] that... it rarely felt like a necessity or obligation.

I enjoyed giving and was always on the lookout for ministries that were impacting the world as well as our city. In 1999 Pam and I got involved in the Spokane Healing Rooms, originally started by John G. Lake in the early 1900s and recently reopened by Cal Pierce in the same location. We could instantly see God's anointing on this ministry. Pam volunteered to help however she could, and we both began praying and serving in the prayer rooms as soon as we could. We saw and heard many wonderful testimonies of people being set free physically and emotionally as God healed them. Cal was anointed to raise an army of ordinary people to do the extraordinary.

I'll never forget seeing a lady months away from dying from an HIV infection being healed after many prayer sessions. Her doctor declared her to be free of HIV, and she is still alive and serving God today. This was happening not just in Spokane. Healing Rooms were opening in many other cities throughout the United States and worldwide. We were excited to support the ministry financially as we could see the potential impact on so many people's lives.

With business air miles, we could travel to conferences with Cal and Michelle and hear many testimonies of what God was doing in this worldwide ministry. We could see God's grace to heal the brokenhearted and do the impossible. From humble beginnings, Spokane Healing Rooms opened up globally, and we felt privileged to be part of what God was doing. He was up to something amazing.

Chuck Pierce (no relation to Cal Pierce), a nationally known prophet, was visiting major cities around the country in 2005 and came to Spokane. That meeting had a great impact on my life. Chuck talked a lot about grace and said we were entering a year of double grace. He was referring to the Hebraic calendar year—we were entering 5765, and it was very significant that there were two 5s, one at the beginning and one at the end. One biblical meaning for the number five is grace. The idea of this next year being a year of double grace got me excited because I had been meditating on 2 Corinthians 9:8 and knew my business success came entirely through God's grace. I also believed that in my weakness His grace was my strength. So a year of double grace sounded amazing.

My faith was ignited, and I wanted to step out and give twice as much as I had ever given. There was no plea for money at this meeting or any presentation of a great need, yet God had put a thought in my head that if it was to be a year of double grace, I could double our giving. I was excited to bless the Healing Rooms with more and see what other ministries I could give to.

However, I first wanted to discuss the idea with Pam because we would have to make some sacrifices. Doubling our giving would be a stretch, and I wanted a confirmation. When I told her what was on my heart, her response went something like this: "I was talking to the Lord recently about how I wanted to be able to give that exact same amount one day. Yes! That would be awesome."

What a confirmation! She didn't hesitate. We were in total agreement. We immediately began increasing our giving as much as possible from our rental properties and salary. We believed our business would have a great year and therefore we would have a bigger bonus to help reach our goal. God had promised to give me the power to get wealth to establish His covenant, and I was all in. I was excited about giving and was fully convinced He would partner with our business to accomplish the impossible.

I rejoiced at the end of that year because our business had risen to a new level. Six of our seven stores had a breakout year. Our seven stores averaged about a $2 million increase in annual sales in the previous seven years. In two of those years we had increased $3.2 million, which was amazing. Yet in this year of double grace, we doubled our best years and increased $6.5 million in sales.

God was faithful to partner with our business, and I believed our employees should prosper just as our company did. Fortunately, we were able to give all our employees bigger bonuses and raises. God anointed our business to handle the increase in sales and care for our customers. We improved our operations and customer service to successfully handle it all. We were breaking records until the recession of 2007–2009, when our sales dropped $7 million over three years. But even then, God's hand was on our business; we did not have to lay anyone off and were still able to make a profit. Our biggest competition in Spokane went out of business, which helped us in the long run. I knew God was anointing everything we were doing as our business rose to a new level.

God saw our hearts' desire to support our church and ministries that impacted the world and He gave us the opportunity to be involved in the Healing Rooms' growth. We were part of the leadership team, and Pam also wrote newsletters with testimonies for the International Association of Healing Rooms so that everyone could hear about what God was doing. The ministry was expanding exponentially, and we were able to support them as well as other ministries. We were living our dream, helping advance God's Kingdom around the world.

DOING THE IMPOSSIBLE

Yes, God loves a cheerful giver. Whatever you give cheerfully and willingly will be given back to you in good measure, pressed down, shaken together, and running over (Luke 6:38).

Everything good comes from God. He blesses what you put your hand to and then multiplies the seed you sow (2 Corinthians 9:10). He is the one who works in you both to will and to do for His good pleasure (Philippians 2:13). He has a plan and purpose for your life, and when you seek Him and tell Him you want to do His will, His part is to do the work with you.

When you open your heart and invite God to partner with you in life, He never leaves or forsakes you. Opening your heart in relationship with

Him is a trust and obedience issue. You need to know that you cannot outgive Him. He multiplies whatever you sow with a good heart.

We were able to double our giving, but the issue isn't really about the amount. It's more about our faith in God and willingness to give freely. He always blesses whatever we put our hand to with faith and a desire to give. I never gave with the expectation of receiving a certain amount of return from Him. All I wanted was God and His partnership in business because I knew I couldn't do it alone.

Is there an area of greater generosity that you want to step into? Purpose in your heart today what you could give finances toward that wouldn't feel like an obligation but would excite you to do. Recall ways you have sown generously in the past and how God was faithful to allow you to reap a return.

This promise is clear in 2 Corinthians 9:8: "God is able to make all grace abound toward you, that you, always having all sufficiency in all things, may have an abundance for every good work." When you are doing a good work that is God's will, you can open your heart and believe for His grace to do the impossible. *All* is mentioned three times in this verse, which means there are no limits on what you can do with God when you know His will.

Some of my most exciting times of giving were when God whispered in my ear and said, "Let's do this together." He told me He would anoint me with His grace if I stepped out of the boat in faith. This giving wasn't always connected to someone taking up an offering or presenting a great need. Often God would come alongside me, nudge me, and say, "This church or ministry."

I have always looked for opportunities to give to ministries that need financing to help launch them to a new level. When we partner with God to support the things on His heart and advance the good news of His beloved Son, it's exciting to see what He does and how many lives are impacted.

> *You need to know you cannot outgive Him. He multiplies whatever you sow with a good heart.*

With a main goal of supporting the gospel, I believed our business was a good work and that God would pour His grace and favor on it. We are told to come boldly to the throne of grace to obtain mercy and find grace in our times of need (Hebrews 4:16). I kept asking for God's grace, and He consistently blessed what we put our hands to. Time after time He was faithful.

TESTIMONY OF HOW GENEROSITY AND FAITH CREATE MULTIPLICATION

Andy Mason's book *God with You at Work* tells the story of Chris, a wood chip buyer for an energy company. Chris needed a miracle to continue generously giving his time on the mission field. He was responsible for ordering and storing wood chips to run a 50-megawatt power plant. Chris and his wife went on a sixteen-day mission trip. Before leaving on this trip, he had sixteen more days of inventory than he needed, yet when he returned, the chip inventory was noticeably down. He found himself praying to God: "If the plant runs out of fuel, my manager will never let me go on a mission trip again."

Chris's wife suggested that he take some plastic gold coins and scatter them over the chip pile as a prophetic act declaring that God, as an abundant provider, would multiply the chips in the pile. Chris did just that, and as he did this, he declared, "God is my provider. He did not pave the way for me to go to Ecuador to see me fail now. He is worthy of being trusted. He promised to supply all my needs and bless me to be a blessing to my employer."

Then things started to happen. First a survey company was employed in May to accurately assess the quantity of chips in the pile for inventory. The survey showed that there were 7,000 tons *more* than what the books showed! For the next two months Chris noticed that even when the chip piles should have been shrinking, they seemed to remain the same size. Another survey was done in June and then in December.

Chris testified to God's goodness:

"All in all, God answered my gold coin prophetic act and extravagantly added $2.2 million worth of chips to my employer's income statement over a ten-month period. I now know that I need never worry about chip supply ever again because God continues to show that He is my abundant provider."

Chris is just an ordinary man who did something extraordinary by stepping out in faith, believing that God is an abundant provider. Through faith, God's grace is more than enough to provide for every good work.

QUESTIONS TO CONSIDER

Are there giving opportunities God is speaking to you about that would bless others in a way that would impact lives with the Kingdom? No matter how radical it may seem, are you willing to step out with Him in faith and believe He can use you to bring much-needed change to the world?

"God is able to make all grace abound toward you, that you, always having all sufficiency in all things, may have an abundance for every good work."

—2 CORINTHIANS 9:8

TRUTH FIFTEEN

God is faithful to provide a way to escape adversity.

"His burden will be taken away from your shoulder, and his yoke from your neck, and the yoke will be destroyed because of the anointing oil."

—ISAIAH 10:27

Even after so many years of being a partner with God, there were times I needed to be reminded that He is always there to fight for me. During one season of significant growth, the stresses and strain of running a business caused me to second-guess our partnership. I still had things to learn about depending on God for all my needs.

After surviving the recession of 2007–2009, we started growing again. Because of our growth, owners of other furniture stores in our region sometimes called to inform us that they were retiring and asked if we wanted to buy their stores. The offers were usually too high and not worth the effort; we would get very little return on our investment.

One offer came from our biggest competitor, who had five stores. They wanted us to buy all their inventory at $1.3 million and pay another $800,000 for the business—over $2 million. It was an excellent opportunity to become dominant in our market. But I felt a check from the Lord, and after much prayer we said no. I did not want to get a large loan from the bank and put the business at risk.

Two years later the same owner called back with a better offer. His company would liquidate all its inventory in a going-out-of-business sale, and all we had to do was take over the leases of the five locations. They owned two locations, and the rents were very reasonable because they were older buildings. The five stores were around 100,000 square feet, and we could simply bring in the same inventory we already carried at our stores. So instead of paying $2.1 million for stores full of furniture, we just took over their leases. They sold all their inventory in a going-out-of-business sale and did very well. We just had to bring furniture from our existing lines to reopen the stores. We would bring in around $1 million of our lines of furniture. This offer was a win for both of us. We still had to open five stores simultaneously but could do it without getting a large loan.

Acquiring five stores at once put a lot of stress on our administrative team. We had always grown one store at a time. That year turned into one of the busiest in the history of our company. We remodeled some of the stores; added new signs, new carpet, and fresh paint; and got ready for inventory to arrive.

Gary hired many of the employees who had worked for the previous owners. They needed to be retrained to work with our computer system and know how our store operated. We had two warehouses now, so we had to manage inventory, transfers, and customer service for two regions. Our sales took off, and our seven original stores started growing too.

To keep everything running smoothly, we all worked a lot of hours. Every day it seemed as if we were putting out fires. We soon realized that our existing 80,000-square-foot warehouse would not be big enough if our sales kept growing. I had the option to buy our existing warehouse, but I also wanted to be able to expand if we needed to, which would require a bigger warehouse. Few warehouses were available because marijuana was legalized in our state, and many older warehouses were bought up as places to grow it.

God knew we had this need, and it soon became clear that He had gone before us. We negotiated an excellent lease in Spokane Valley at an industrial park. They built us new offices exactly as we needed them. We leased a 120,000-square-foot warehouse with the option to add another 30,000 square feet. In addition to the new office, they made many improvements to accommodate our needs. There was adequate room to grow.

The expansion had already put a lot of stress on our administrative staff to maintain great customer service and keep everything running smoothly. Now we had to move our entire warehouse and set up a new office. We began strategizing how to move over $2 million of inventory from our old warehouse to the new warehouse over one week—around two hundred trucks of furniture, or forty trucks a day.

We had only eight delivery trucks, so everyone had to stop their regular activity and help with the move. This would also involve stopping the normal flow of inventory to our warehouse for about a week.

We planned to be ready to continue operations at the end of the week; otherwise, we might have a logjam of inventory in our new receiving area. We also had to start a new system of barcoding every piece of furniture in our warehouse to increase the flow of goods dramatically. Though this would greatly help with tracking our inventory, it could slow down the whole process. But we wanted to do things right from the beginning.

One month before we were going to move, some giant obstacles came up. We quickly realized we couldn't move the racking from our old warehouse until the furniture on the racks was moved. Then, because of the extra square footage, when the furniture was moved over to the new warehouse, we needed new racks to put furniture on for barcoding. So we needed to find racks and have them installed in time, and we also needed to hire a team to take the old racks apart and install them at our new warehouse as soon as possible.

Our office moving date was another issue. My controller told me she had ordered the wiring for our computer system to be installed by a specific date so we could move our office over and start barcoding all the furniture. But the installers couldn't guarantee the date, which could set the installation off by a week.

I was being presented with potential problems for which I could not control the outcome. There were so many unknown factors. But the obstacles reached a tipping point a few days later. My controller, who was also my computer expert, walked into my office and told me she had been offered a new job and would be moving to a different city one week before our big move. I had been depending on her to oversee the office and our new barcoding system at the new warehouse. I was trying to build a team around my son-in-law to run the company for the next twenty years, and I thought our controller was key to our future.

I think I slept a total of twelve hours that week. I couldn't think about anything but the huge obstacles I had no solutions for. Who would run the office? Would we be able to do everything in a week? I felt trapped and started doubting my decision to expand. I questioned whether I had mistakenly expanded too fast from pride. Was God still with me? Was I experiencing burnout? Was my business going to implode from growing too fast?

> *God showed that He is faithful.*

Desperate to sleep better, I asked my doctor for sleep medicine and was given anxiety medicine instead. Instead of working, the medication just made me more anxious. I was advised to stay away from work, which also didn't help. My faith was at an all-time low because I looked at the circumstances and questioned whether God was still with me. Had pride led me to disobey by getting ahead of His plans? Was this expansion putting too much pressure on our employees?

I was focused on all the potential problems, not on God's faithfulness to fulfill His promises, including His promise never to leave or forsake me. I believed the lies of the enemy. I felt weak and incapable of doing anything about our company's situation.

In many ways I felt like Gideon hiding in the winepress, questioning where God was. In his story an angel showed up and told him to go in God's might to save Israel.

God showed up for me too. Even "if we are faithless, He remains faithful" (2 Timothy 2:13). In one of the darkest moments of my life, He prompted two different people to call and encourage me.

These people lived hundreds of miles away in different states and had no idea of what was happening in my life. One was Shirley. We had known her and her husband for years, but she always talked to Pam when she called. This time she called me because, she said, the Lord had prompted her to encourage me. She didn't know why, but she sensed that He wanted her to tell me that He loved me and that I had a special purpose before Him. Not long afterward, David called from California and said almost the same thing. I had to stop believing the lie that God was no longer partnered with me.

God showed that He was faithful, of course. Our warehouse move was successful, and our office manager became our controller and did a fantastic job immediately. She was calm and to this day handles problems without telling me about them unless I need to know. That warehouse has been a blessing as our company has grown, and we now have 220,000 square feet to handle our increased sales.

God's anointing took the burden off me and broke the yoke around my neck. He is our Redeemer, our Savior. Jesus gave His life to make us whole in every area of our lives.

When life seems to be falling apart with problems and obstacles everywhere you look, remember that God is with you to redeem your life. When you turn to Him and partner with Him, He fights for you. He will always strengthen and help you when you're in trouble.

RE-EXAMINING OUR HEARTS

When we co-labor with God, we may not feel like it in the moment, but we always have more than enough to overcome our circumstances. When we stop focusing on the storm and turn toward Him, we receive His truth and His promises. He is always there, ready to fight for us. Our faith is strengthened when we remember what He has done for us. Believing and confessing His promises connects us to His resurrection power. He redeemed our lives from dead and fruitless works so that we can continually overcome obstacles and live in fruitful works.

God's promise to Joshua applies to all who place their faith in Him: "I will be with you. I will not leave you nor forsake you. Be strong and of good courage" (Joshua 1:5–6). Jesus promised those who labored with heavy burdens that they could come to Him and find rest (Matthew 11:28). God is always faithful to fulfill His promises for those who partner with Him.

It is very easy to get so wrapped up in succeeding (or not failing) that we develop a fear of failing. I looked at all the things that could go wrong and tried to prevent them. I should have been looking instead at my partner and His promises. Through His promises, we can participate in His divine nature; walk in His Kingdom of righteousness, peace, and joy; and fulfill our purpose and destiny.

During this critical time I had to re-examine my heart. Was I still believing God's promises that we were partners in this business? Had I forgotten all He had done for me? Did I know, regardless of the circumstances, that Jesus was my Provider, Protector, and Savior?

When all the obstacles to our move seemed overwhelming, I had to examine my heart and ask forgiveness for focusing on the problems rather than on God. He is the one with all the solutions. I believed a lie that He had left me because I had disobeyed or made a bad decision to expand too much and that everything would fall apart.

The truth was much different. God was still my partner in business, and He is always faithful. I asked for help to rebuild my faith and to believe in His anointing to break the yoke around my neck trying to hold me back.

The reality was that God had prepared my company for moments like that. I learned to rejoice and remember all He had supernaturally done for us. He armed our business for that battle. With very little help from me, our distribution center is now thriving and excelling at double the volume of our old warehouse. That experience made me even more determined not to turn back but to continue moving forward to fulfill my purpose of financing the gospel around the world.

I've realized that my destiny in God is not dependent on the company's success year by year. It's dependent on believing that He is the Christ and always remembering His promises in my heart.

A QUOTE ON EXAMINING YOUR FAITH

If we don't tune ourselves up and recalibrate daily, we'll drift off course. A very small drift may not seem like much, but by the end of your life, it might mean that you missed your destiny, which was God's best plan for you. Larger drifts, of course, could get you fired from your job or cooling your heels in prison. All sorts of bad things happen when we don't recalibrate ourselves to run in sync with our maker. (Michael L. Galiga, *Win Every Battle: Conquering Fear and Claiming Victory for Success in Life*)

QUESTIONS TO CONSIDER

What setbacks have you faced that caused you to question yourself or God? Did you find ways to reconnect your heart and mind to the truth that God didn't walk away from you? What is your success truly dependent on?

"Examine yourselves as to whether you are in the faith.
Test yourselves. Do you not know yourselves, that Jesus Christ is in you?"

—2 CORINTHIANS 13:5

TRUTH SIXTEEN

God promises that if you come to Him, He will give you rest.

"Come to me, all you who labor and are heavy laden, and I will give you rest. Take my yoke upon you and learn of Me, for I am gentle and lowly in heart, and you will find rest for your souls."

—MATTHEW 11:28–29

Rest comes when you are yoked with Jesus, walking in His strength and promises. And walking with God in business has been an amazing adventure. We started with nothing, and God partnered with us to fulfill His plans and purposes for our lives. Writing this book has been a great experience of remembering how faithful He has been in blessing what we put our hands to and helping us overcome many difficult situations.

God has always been with me. He has never left me. When I sought Him with all my heart, He was always there. Even when my faith failed, He was still with me—as if He didn't see my failures. Together we overcame many impossible situations I could never have handled in my own strength and ability.

God blessed our furniture business and real estate investments. We have seen our business grow to fourteen stores and more than two hundred dedicated employees, with sales over $70 million a year and no debt.

It all started with believing in my heart, confessing, and acting on one promise from Deuteronomy 8:18—that God would give me the power to get wealth to establish His covenant. He truly opened the windows of heaven and poured out a blessing we could not contain. Most importantly, we have been able to financially support important ministries that have significantly impacted many lives around the world.

God prompted me to start implementing an exit plan—to turn the company over to my son-in-law, Adam, and then retire. He had worked at Walker's for over ten years, and I had slowly been turning most of my duties over to him and our administration team. I spent most of my time looking at reports, answering questions, and affirming their decisions. I wanted to spend more quality time with Pam in this next season of our lives, and we were excited to see what God still had in store for us. We were both looking forward to a change He had been telling us was coming.

Then COVID-19 hit, and all our stores were closed. The lockdown measures helped me decide that it was time to cut back dramatically. God had been trying to prepare me, and suddenly I was put in more of a consultant role.

Adam had excellent computer skills. He quickly set up our website so we could sell online. Our stores were forced to close temporarily, yet we couldn't stop the flow of furniture coming into our distribution center. Our warehouse quickly overflowed, and bills piled up with no money coming in. Our business savings account was being depleted. Hard decisions had to be made.

We temporarily laid everyone off until our stores could reopen. As before, all I could see and hear were the problems we were facing, and there seemed to be few solutions other than praying and waiting to see when stores could reopen. But I knew I could trust God to protect us and provide solutions for our company and employees.

It was time to let Adam take over. I retired, became more of an off-site consultant, and turned my business over to him. I would be involved only in major decisions. God had been preparing Adam for this, and I could see that he was well able to take our company through the pandemic.

The whole world was shaken. The news was full of economic crises, and many feared the future. People were discouraged, upset, and losing hope. There were lockdowns and closures of supposedly "non-essential" businesses. There were layoffs and all kinds of mandates on what we could and could not do. Long freight delays with inventory and part shortages caused a dramatic increase in customer problems and a loss of business. Then there were labor shortages aggravated by people not showing up for work after having been offered a job. Daily negative news about what was going wrong and who was at fault bombarded people's lives. It was hard to know what to do. Everything was changing so fast.

Retiring from work was one thing, but I never intended to retire from my purpose. I was going to continue running my race to win, to fulfill my destiny and my promise of financing ministries to proclaim the name of Jesus around the world. True rest comes from partnering with God to fulfill your purpose. I had a lot more time, so I spent much of it pressing into Jesus and waiting on Him, reading, praying, and worshiping more than I ever had, receiving His strength.

All the dire news weakened my faith, so I wanted to strengthen it. I turned to His Word and held on to His promises. I rejoiced and gave glory to Him for what He had done and was going to do. Instead of focusing on the negative circumstances impacting the world, I spent a lot of time reading and meditating on God's report. There were so many things He had done for me and our business that I could remember.

In moments of weakness and doubt, I kept pressing into His presence, running to Him, learning from Him, and receiving His grace, peace, and joy. I spent a lot more time listening to prophetic voices like Johnny Enlow and others on social media who had words of encouragement.

Jesus sacrificed His life to give us a better covenant with better promises. Our inheritance includes access to the throne of grace, where we can live with Christ while walking on the earth. We are in alliance with the King of kings, and all His resources—His protection, provision, wisdom, direction, and presence—are available to us. His will is for all to know Him, "from the least of them to the greatest of them" (Hebrews 8:11). Through His amazing promises in the Bible, we get to partner with Him in life.

During difficult times we must remember all the times God has turned bad situations into good ones. We have to rejoice in those moments where He helped us through situations in which we couldn't see the answer. Always thank Him for His faithfulness and continue believing in His goodness.

Over the years there have been so many times when I did not know how circumstances would go, but I was determined to praise Him and rejoice in our partnership, even during bad times. I can't imagine how I would have handled all these difficulties without partnering with God in my business.

ALL THINGS ARE POSSIBLE WITH GOD

Nothing that happens in our business, in our economy, or our lives can separate us from God's love and His promises. Father God, Jesus, and the Holy Spirit desire to fellowship (partner) with us.

Jesus came to earth, demonstrated God's love, and then gave His life on the cross so we could gain access to fellowship with God. The Greek word for *fellowship* is *koinonia,* which means "partnership, participation, intimacy, or communion." Our lives are transformed as we walk with God in relationship with Him and believe His promises. And it's a choice.

Wherever you are in life, no matter what you've done or how you've failed, God will pour His love into you when you turn to Him. When you give your life to Jesus and walk with Him, He gives you His life. God's plan from the beginning was to partner with people to raise them out of their circumstances, giving glory to His Son so that the world would know He sent His Son, Jesus.

> *As we walk with God in relationship with Him and believe His promises, our lives are transformed. And it's a choice.*

I've discovered that blessing the Lord and rejoicing in our partnership activates our faith and increases our fellowship or communion together. No matter how bad the circumstances appear, everything goes more smoothly when we rejoice over being in this situation together. I often remind myself of Paul's example of singing and worshiping the Lord in his prison cell at night. From all appearances, it was one of the worst days of his life, yet he enthusiastically fellowshipped with God without focusing on his circumstances. He didn't know what would happen but knew he wanted to fellowship with God. Then God showed up with an earthquake. Paul's chains fell off, and he walked out of prison. Awed by what he saw, the prison guard was saved, along with his family. Rejoicing opens the door to receiving what God wants to do in our lives.

God's Word is one of the greatest weapons for defeating the enemy and overcoming obstacles. When we rejoice over God's will and have a revelation of a promise in our hearts, nothing is impossible with Him. Romans 10:17 says that faith comes by hearing (in our minds) and hearing by the Word of God (in our hearts). When we start seeing and confessing a promise, we begin stepping out in faith to believe and receive from God. Our words and actions reveal what we really believe in our hearts.

Our lives will be transformed when we take a promise and sow it into our hearts as an absolute truth. As we develop a lifestyle of partnering with Him, the revelation of God's promise in our hearts becomes established in our lives.

I had to cease trying to solve all these major problems in my strength. Instead, I needed to rest in God's promises and faithfulness to fulfill His promises to our company. I had to rest in God's plan to turn the business over to Adam and our administration team. Breakthrough came when I believed the unseen realm and the truth of God's promises instead of the visible realm of bad circumstances and all the possibilities of things going wrong. I had to reestablish core values and beliefs in my heart, remembering how faithful God had been and expecting Him to direct Adam as He directed me. God would be faithful to give Adam solutions to problems.

My wife reminded me that whatever happens with the business will not change the truth that God is with us to fulfill our destiny and that we both need to simply trust God with our business completely,

When impossible situations arise, rejoice in how faithfully God fulfills His promises. When we can't see any solutions, rejoice that all things are possible with God. Spend more time believing His promises in the unseen realm instead of the circumstances of the visible realm.

After the lockdown things started changing. We had record-breaking sales from pent-up demand. We rested in God's promises and His love, and we had breakthrough that was impossible in our own strength.

Rejoicing in God and His goodness brings breakthrough. That's what happened with Paul when he was singing and praying after one of the worst days of his life. Paul had learned to rejoice and boast in his trials because then the power of Christ would rest on Him. He said he took pleasure in infirmities, reproaches, needs, persecutions, and distresses for Christ's sake, "for when I am weak, then I am strong" (2 Corinthians 12:10). He had developed a lifestyle of worshiping and praising God regardless of circumstances. And God responded by breaking his chains and opening prison doors (Acts 16:25–26). Thanksgiving opens the door to receiving from God, and praise activates our faith to walk with Him at a higher level.

On the other hand, fear, complaining, blaming, anger, and bitterness will prevent our ability to receive from God. I had to take fearful and worrisome thoughts captive and reestablish His Word in my heart, believing and receiving His promises. For most of my life, when trials came, I rejoiced that God was with me and that we were in this together. I thanked Jesus for giving me access to the Father to receive His abundance of grace to help in times of trouble.

Rejoicing in God and His goodness brings breakthrough.

During those times of distress, I had to return to my core values. I remembered all that God had done for me and rejoiced that He was faithful to fulfill His promises. I knew that "all things work together for the good to those who love God, to those who are the called according to His purpose" (Romans 8:28). I set my mind to fulfilling my purpose in Him, giving generously to ministries to help establish His gospel, rejoicing and expecting that my Redeemer would always be with me. The only thing I wanted to fear was the possibility of hindering my relationship with Him and stepping out of my destiny.

David wrote Psalm 34 when he was at a very low point, and I'm sure it influenced Paul generations later:

> I will bless the Lord at all times;
> His praise shall continually be in my mouth.
> My soul shall make its boast in the Lord;
> The humble shall hear of it and be glad.
> Oh, magnify the Lord with me,
> And let us exalt His name together.
> I sought the Lord, and He heard me,
> And delivered me from all my fears. (Psalm 34:1–4)

As the world gets darker, purpose in your heart to magnify the Lord, exalt His name, and bless Him at all times, no matter what is happening in your life. Choose to see His victory and believe His plans and purposes will come to pass. I am a long way from always doing this, but the more I rejoice and bless God, the more I seem to be entering into His rest and peace.

Pam and I are so humbled by the faithfulness of God's love toward us. I believe, and have seen it proven in our lives, that you can't outgive God. Financially and in other ways, we received resources from heaven as Jesus described them—pressed down, shaken together, and running over! God has been so faithful to reward us with increase and multiplication.

This goes well beyond monetary resources. We've seen great favor and grace on the lives of our family members and employees. God's hedge of protection and provision has been very apparent. With thankful hearts we give all glory to our Papa God.

A QUOTE ON ENTERING HIS REST

We need to enter into the rest God has prepared for us. We need to learn how to become a resting place for Him to dwell. We need to become a temple where God is always invited to come and pour His oil into our lives. The good news is that, at all times, God is ready to pour it freely over all who desire it. (Heidi Baker, *Birthing the Miraculous: The Power of Personal Encounters with God to Change Your Life and the World*)

QUESTIONS TO CONSIDER

Are you committed to a lifestyle of partnering with Him? What can you do differently to stay in fellowship with Him? Are there any specific promises God has revealed that you realize you must establish your life or business upon?

What would it look like for you to personally enter into the rest of God in your business challenges? How can you maintain that mentality of rest rather than striving in your own strength?

When you get to the season of life when you can let go of your business, how do you want to be able to describe the partnership you've had with God? "We have access by faith into this grace in which we stand, and rejoice in hope of the glory of God" (Romans 5:2).

"There remains therefore a rest for the people of God. For he who has entered His rest has himself also ceased from his works as God did from His. Let us therefore be diligent to enter that rest."

—HEBREWS 4:9–11

CONCLUSION

By Johnny Enlow

Mark and Pam began living out their calling without a business but with a deep desire to advance God's Kingdom. It's easy to look at all the advantages they didn't have: no huge inheritance, no investors initially lined up to get them up and running, no established business model, not even an idea of what business they should start. They only had a dream to advance the gospel of the Kingdom further and a conviction that God would keep His promises. But they did have a huge advantage that no one would have noticed at first—a God advantage. They followed biblical principles, listened to God's leading, took steps of faith, and experienced God's blessing.

You likely picked up on many of the golden nuggets of truth that Mark has shared throughout his story. One of the biggest is the "starter dough" for this ministry of wealth—the initial $5,000 gift he was given, how he used that to bless others, and how he then received even more. Right from the start he demonstrated that he would be a channel of blessing through whom God's resources could flow.

That kind of faith separates the "wannabes" from the "real deals." God saw the real deal in Mark and built a partnership with him that has produced much fruit over nearly five decades. Mark's partnership with God manifested in many ways over all those years and demonstrates how God wants to grow and develop trusted ministers of wealth.

This purpose was evident early in the ministry of Jesus. His first public miracle was not about supernatural healing or deliverance. It was a miracle of provision (John 2:1–10). The hosts of a wedding would have suffered huge embarrassment by running out of wine, so Mary urged Jesus to do something about it. That's lesson number one in the Mountain of Economy. If you have a sudden need, bring it to Jesus. He understands celebrations, social conventions, and especially weddings. He also knows how to provide when His people ask. Jesus is never restricted by what people don't have; He always uses what people *do* have.

Let that sink in. When you partner with God in business—or in anything else—focus on what you *do* have, not what you don't have. Jesus can feed thousands with a few loaves and fishes, even seating everyone to eat before there was food. He can provide a huge catch of fish if you have a net to drop into the water wherever He says to drop it, no matter how unlikely it is. And he can fill six empty waterpots with wine when someone gives Him some water to work with. When you partner with Jesus in business, expect His instructions to be counterintuitive. Wisdom from God often seems foolish to human beings.

We don't know exactly when the water turned to wine, but we do know it took a step of faith.

The servants had to fill the pots with water, as Jesus said, and they had to take it to the master of the feast to taste before they or the hosts even knew what it would taste like. As it turned out, the master was impressed at the hosts' brilliant plan of bringing out the best wine last, contrary to custom. And since the six waterpots held up to thirty gallons each, this wonderful wine was essentially an endless supply. The whole town could join in.

God's provision is extravagant. He is not the God of "just enough." He is the God of "pressed down, shaken together, and running over" (Luke 6:38). He is the God who not only feeds five thousand but also leaves twelve full baskets of leftovers when everyone has eaten.

We see a common sequence of events in many of Jesus's miracles, beginning with a basic truth:

1. Jesus considers everything ministry.
2. Identify your need.
3. Bring that need to Jesus.
4. He will ask what you have rather than focus on what you don't have.
5. Follow His special instructions, which are usually counterintuitive.
6. Enjoy the miracle.
7. Steward the testimony by telling it.

This is what Mark and Pam repeatedly did during their years of service in business. They offered what they had, and again and again they saw God come through for them. They have celebrated many miracles and stewarded the testimonies well. In fact, this book is one way of magnifying those testimonies—and testimonies proclaimed become prophecies of what God can do in the lives of those who believe He will repeat the miracle.

Many of us need a healed perspective in this area. For far too long, Christians have had an orphan perspective in the area of provision—a distorted perception of God as the "barely enough" or "only the most basic needs" God. But God, our Provider, is looking for those who can handle the immense provision He wants to pour out on His people, not for self-centered consumption but for Kingdom purposes. He is calling many to have a "channel" mentality rather than a "reservoir" mentality—to let His resources flow not only to them but *through* them. He wants these financial stewards to pursue wealth, not to accumulate it but to *give* it.

When your mind and spirit operate in that kind of thinking, as Mark and Pam's do, you are in a position for God the Provider to trust you with financial resources. I've heard people tell me excitedly how much they want to give—not how much they want to make, but how much they want to bless others and advance God's Kingdom. When that's your heart and you demonstrate that with what you already have, God can trust you with overflow. That's the kind of wealth that, according to Proverbs 10:22, comes without sorrow.

If you are called to the Mountain of Economy, let Mark and Pam serve as a model for how to pursue Kingdom finances for Kingdom purposes. If you are called to another mountain of society, let their example inspire you to think out of the box and partner with God to bring Kingdom influence into your work, whatever it may be. Whatever your assignment from God is, He wants you to trust Him for provision and opportunities.

Your business is a holy work. It's a powerful way to support ministries that are advancing the Kingdom, but it's even more than that. Your business is a ministry. Pursue your calling with that heart, and God will show up for you just as He has for Mark, Pam, and many others who have applied His Word, listened for His voice, followed His leading, and believed in His goodness. God isn't asking you to carry the heavy burden of your business. He enjoys the opportunity of being your business partner. For Him, it's always ultimately about relationship. So dare to believe that He cares about you and solving societal problems—through you, your business, and the finances that come from it.

And remember: whatever obstacles you face on your Kingdom adventure, all things are possible with God's truths at work in you and through you.